Praise for *One Ripple at a Time*

"*One Ripple at a Time* is about loss but also how to move into the future, how to gather what is left and forge forward."

— **Marisela Rizik, author of *Of Forgotten Times***

"Her truth helps guide others to hold compassionate space with grief they've hidden away and ultimately find themselves again."

—**Katie Joy Duke, author of *Still Breathing: My Journey with Love, Loss, and Reinvention***

"What appears to be a heartbreaking story turns out to be one of resilience and triumph over unspeakable tragedy. Life can still be beautiful after your worst nightmare."

—**Jillian Smith, author**

"Janice bravely guides us through the moment her son is lost and finds courage to face her fears, protect her family, and overcome the trauma."

—**Joanne De Simone, author of *Fall and Recovery: Raising Children with Disabilities through Lessons Learned in Dance***

"Janice's journey to reclaim her lost child and the love they shared is filled with tenderness and courage. This book glows with strength and wisdom."

—**Mary Bauer, author of *Mercury, Miko, and Me***

One Ripple at a Time

A Mother's Story of Life After Loss

Janice Jensen

SHE WRITES PRESS

Published 2024
Printed in the United States of America
Print ISBN: 978-1-64742-794-8
E-ISBN: 978-1-64742-795-5
Library of Congress Control Number: 2024909091

For information, address:
She Writes Press
1569 Solano Ave #546
Berkeley, CA 94707

Interior Design by Kiran Spees

She Writes Press is a division of SparkPoint Studio, LLC.

Names and identifying characteristics have been changed to protect the privacy of certain individuals.

For my daughter who conquered every ripple with me
And for Brian's enduring love

June 20, 1972

We were a family of four with boundless spirit.
Alarm about the future was a fleeting mist.
Until it wasn't.

ONE
CHOICES

Vapor rose through black alder and hazel trees toward the Alps while the sleepy eel Inn River wound east along the Inn Valley. Nine-year-old Brian pressed binoculars against the car window for a closer look. "I see it! We can find pretty rocks."

My husband, Oskar, turned into the auto repair shop southwest of Innsbruck for our Volkswagen's first factory-authorized servicing. Fifteen days earlier, we had traveled from Oregon to Wolfsburg, Germany, to take delivery of the Squareback and visit the storied Bremen Town Musicians statue, the Nuremberg Transport Museum, and Bavarian castles. Our plan included dancing at Austrian music festivals and hiking in the Alps.

The ignition off, Oskar grinned at our two children. "Let's have fun today." Brian, with the fair skin tone and expressions of his Norwegian-born father, jumped out and ran behind the building to find the river. Peeking through a birch tree at the top of the hill, he motioned to six-year-old Erika and said, "I can teach you to skip stones."

Morning sun filtered through the canopy, the binoculars disclosing a peaceful stream about fifteen feet wide. A few medium-sized boulders with two or three large ones lay scattered midbank, while smaller rocks and sand merged with the hill. Several orange-breasted chaffinches flew between trees in the woods. They seemed to trill a welcome.

Early for the appointment, Oskar confirmed the start time, then suggested a short hike to check out the river. The four of us flattened brush at the top of the hill, and when tree limbs and bushes got in the way of the tromp down the primitive switchbacks, the kids and their father swiped branches aside for me.

I heard my son humming phrases from Mozart's Sonata in C Major, his favorite piano music. He had recently practiced the first lines of melody on his recorder and played them for us. In two days, we would visit the composer's museum in Salzburg, where the prodigy had lived.

Rounding the last corner, I stood at the top of the hill and scanned the area below for hazards, my usual ritual in a new setting. I watched Oskar study the river and landscape. After we nodded in agreement that it looked safe, my husband clambered down the muddy incline with the kids. They jumped over smaller standing boulders and around larger ones toward the slow glide some sixty feet ahead.

When my feet touched the loose stones, my mind flashed to me as a seven-year-old, knee-deep in a lake, slipping on moss and clutching my shivering body. Small waves had made me afraid I would drown. This river was causing a shiver too familiar, and I started to run back to the car. I stopped and closed my eyes, willing myself to breathe deeply. *You're here for your children. Stay.* Scrambling over the rocks to stand with the kids beside the flow, I caught a sweet but unfamiliar fragrance.

Brian crouched and picked up a pebble with pinkish flecks. Oskar, an amateur rock hound, called it feldspar, while Erika pushed falling hair across her freckles to lean close. She gave her father a missing-tooth grin and tilted the rock until it sparkled.

Thinking about our wait while the car was being serviced, I panned the binoculars left and right once again: normal-looking dry area with a few stumps, small stream, and no sticks floating. No signs saying DANGER or KEEP OUT, which made the probe feel accurate. Oskar joined me, and we confirmed that lunch by the water would be a treat.

I motioned both children to the area midway between the hill and the stream with smaller standing rocks, a couple of larger boulders, and a bed of pebbles. Placing one hand on each child's shoulder, I looked straight into their eyes and directed a finger toward the ground. Marveling at how his sky-blue eyes matched his shirt, I kissed Brian's forehead and said, "Yes, you can collect pretty rocks. Find your treasures here, away from the river. When I return, you can practice skipping stones."

Brian said, "Got it, Mom."

Erika said, "Okay."

The children jumped and clapped, then squatted and pored over pebbles. "Be safe, and I'll be right back." I saw them glance at me with visions of cheese sandwiches and apple slices dancing in their eyes while I sprinted up the hill. Halfway, I caught up to Oskar, scanned the river, and listened. Everything appeared calm.

At the top of the slope, I leaped over blackberry bushes toward the car while Oskar headed for the office. Stuffing food into the picnic basket, I set it on the pavement, grabbed the water jug, and sprinted back down the path. My previous day's journal entry flashed before me: *Brian and Erika asked to skip breakfast and get on with music festivals and hikes.* I loved their curiosity. I also trusted them to follow directions, even when they would rather not. The steep hill and sharp downward turns made it easy to hurry, but a quarter of the way, I peered at the bank and checked on the kids. Still in the safety zone, they were picking up small rocks and stashing a few in their pockets. Erika waved a hand high to her brother. I imagined her saying, "This rock is the prettiest in the whole world."

Oskar passed me and pushed ahead. Halfway, still willing my legs to hurry, I tripped over tubers and vines, then hunched at the side of a black alder to watch Brian. Amazed at his ability to find both pretty rocks and flat stones, I saw him stuff several into each pocket. *He's getting ready to teach Erika how to skip.* Reaching for the binoculars to get a better look, I discovered they were left behind.

Two steps farther, I squinted and blinked. It appeared that my son was standing closer to the stream than the distance we had settled on. A few paces later, I wedged myself between two trunks and saw him kneeling beside a large boulder in the approved area. Water crawled just feet from its far side. *How did the water get there?*

Strength drained from my arms. Brian hadn't gone nearer to the river.

The river had come nearer to him.

I leaped straight down through the bushes and vines towards where I saw Erika kneeling, lifting pebbles from her pocket, and stowing them next to a medium-sized boulder a bit downstream and closer to the bank.

"We'll be right there," I shouted.

"Brian! Erika!"

"Oskar!" I yelled.

My husband was a switchback ahead. Why didn't he answer? I dropped the jug, raced through the brush, and fell against his shoulder. He stopped singing his Norwegian folk song.

I thrust my arm toward the river. "Get the kids!"

Seconds later, loud tumbles riddled my ears when upstream water rushed the area below. *Oh, my God!*

What we didn't know—and couldn't have known—was that across the border, the Swiss power company had opened dams, releasing this torrent into the channel that held our children.

Oskar glanced below, dropped the picnic basket, and bolted between the trees. I ran behind him and screamed, "Hurry!" while I stumbled over roots. Glimpses of the kids showed them still crouched near our side of the boulders. At a large opening, maybe twenty feet from the edge of the hill, I gasped and screamed, "No!" as water lapped around both sides of Brian's rock.

"Go to the hill," I hollered and tripped, grabbing a tree.

"Go to the hill *now*!" Oskar yelled above the churning current.

God, let our children hear us.

At the top of the incline, I saw Brian stand, silt-filled water washing over his shoes. By the time I clambered and slipped down the mud, the river was licking at Erika's sneakers. It swirled around Brian's.

I called, "I'm coming!" and saw my son climb to the top of his boulder. Erika watched her brother and hoisted herself onto a flat part of hers. Both kids pressed their knees to their chins as the water rose more quickly by the second. The surge had only begun short minutes ago, but it had become a deluge.

Oskar plunged toward Erika on the smaller, closer boulder, the rising current pushing at his calves, then his knees and waist, while a strong wave pushed against Brian's rock.

I watched a scroll of water toss Erika into the river.

Our son turned to his father, his little face registering fear.

He called, "Save Erika," as his sister started to float downstream.

Oskar lost his footing, then swam toward his daughter, grasping one arm.

"Hold on!" I called to our son as I ran into the river. My sneakers slid on underwater stones, the flow rising to my calves. I flailed my arms for balance, but the force started to carry me downriver. *I don't know how to swim.* I locked my hands around the sharp top of a protruding rock, certain I would drown if I let go. I looked at Brian.

I have to get to my son.

Brian slid but gripped a knob and pulled his chin and chest toward the front of the boulder while the unbridled water cascaded backward under his knees.

A stronger wave slammed against his rock and shot skyward.

I froze.

Half-swimming and gaining footing, Oskar pulled Erika from under the deep water.

A split-second of serenity seemed to surround my son.

When the falling force slapped full strength against his body, it wrenched him from the rock into the glacial flow. Another wave hit and propelled him downstream. I screamed, barely catching a glimpse of Brian floating out of sight.

Oskar drew Erika close and clutched a trunk. I saw her cry, showing she could breathe again.

The rampant waves drenched me as I scrambled to get to my husband who was now feet from the hill. "I can't move," I yelled.

"Squat, stretch your arms out, and inch each foot," he called out. I did and squeezed anything that held me for a second. I stepped one heavy sneaker at a time toward him. At his back, my hands bled down the khaki pants as we pushed our soaked bodies to the vertical roots. Erika wrapped herself tighter around her father's chest.

Trying to hold tangled foliage at the clay wall, I lost my grip and stumbled until I could grab another outgrowth. There was no way to shield our ears against the sound of the rising water that continued its crashes and slams downstream.

*   *

Erika dropped a leg from her father's waist. "I have to get Brian," she said.

I turned my head toward my husband's ashen face while he lifted his daughter to my back. He kissed her and said, "I'm going to find your brother," starting downstream amid the thundering water rising above our calves.

Aghast, I blurted, "Climb up to the hill!" He glanced at the flow and managed to step on small clumps of mud and rock and hoist himself to the edge of the slope. I saw him tramp through brush and around trees facing the river, loudly exclaiming, "Brian!" I wanted more than anything to keep Erika with me and run along the ridge shouting, "We're here, my son!" He could be clinging to a branch somewhere.

My daughter's small frame shuddered in her soggy shirt and shorts as she closed her arms tight at my neck. Determined to get her into dry clothes quickly, I pointed myself up the muddy roots.

TWO
WHERE IS BRIAN?

Erika clawed at my neck and cried, "Mom, don't let me fall!" Promising to keep her safe, I jabbed my feet and grabbed roots with knobs until I planted spongy shoes on trailing vines. Wriggling to the ground, Erika ran to the first switchback and stood shivering, her arms crossed.

I steadied my legs and hurried to her. Pressing my face against her shirt, I said, "Thank you for being so brave."

We huffed through upturns to the grassy area at the back of the repair shop. I cried out for help. Mechanic Alois ran out an open door, and I said, "My son—in the river!" He and his partner raced down the slope.

Erika wrapped her trembling body around me. Holding her close, I kissed her, told her it was good three people were searching, and carried her to the car. The sweltering interior felt welcoming, and at the back seat, she raised her arms for her shirt to come off, then pushed her cutoff jeans down. I pulled the plaid blanket to our necks, and she blinked several times while I rubbed her blue legs. She said, "Brian is waving, 'I'm right here.'"

My daughter settled on my lap; I tucked her head close and squeezed my eyelids while dread flashed to the tremendous slam of water and rocks. I wanted to hope my son was waiting somewhere on a log and said to Erika, "Your dad will look everywhere, and your big brother will fight with all his might to get to him."

She rejected warming up in her comfy red sweater, instead choosing the blue-striped shirt Brian had worn two days earlier when we hiked lower trails in the Alps. "Until Dad brings him back," she said.

I bundled the blanket close to her and slid away to open the hatch. After pulling out a wool sweater to cover my soggy shoulders, I lifted my son's blue shirt and sketchpad from the top of his suitcase. I hugged them both and prayed he was waiting on a stump, signaling, "I'm right here."

I felt a strong urge to go down to the river, run along the bank, and inspect every log and boulder. At the same time, I shook like jelly and struggled to close the hatch. Next to Erika again, I slipped her brother's shirt over her head, and she pulled up her striped pants. Nestling her against me, I rocked her like I was trying to win a race. She pushed away until I sat still.

Whispering a rhythmic cadence, "You're safe, and I love you now and forever," helped us both breathe deeply and slow the shock. A clear voice said, *Stay with your daughter.*

This was, of course, for her benefit—Erika had to trust me—but it was for mine, too. A part of me was scared of what I might find.

At that time in western Austria, no official rescue team existed, leaving the police to conduct the search. Three officers arrived at one o'clock, and I repeated to myself several times, *Oskar and the others will peer at every possible rock, piece of wood, and clump of vegetation.*

When both of us were warmer, I asked Erika if she would enjoy eating a snack under a nearby maple tree. She folded the blanket while I picked up a small water jug from the trunk and a container of nuts, raisins, and animal crackers.

The blanket spread, she sorted through the canister for her favorites and leaned against my chest. I wrapped my arms around her and rocked gently while she chewed.

"Mom, how come Dad saved me and not Brian?"

"You were closest."

The words numbed me to the core, but then another thought let me breathe. The big wave had struck her brother seconds before she was pulled to her father's chest. Although Brian would have seen Erika lifted from under the water, she had surely been spared the image of him flying off his rock.

Later, I shared another thought about the words, *Save Erika.* "Sometimes things just happen." I told her life can be that way, but I believed her brother loved her "with his very best love." She smoothed the front of the blue shirt and snuggled closer.

With the last patch of shade gone, Erika climbed off my lap, wiped her forehead on a shirtsleeve, and said, "Brian does that." I dabbed my eyes while she filled her mouth three more times.

2:00 p.m.

"How about we go inside where it's cooler," I said, standing to gather our belongings.

At the repair shop entrance, I fumbled with the knob, knowing if I turned it, I might learn that Brian was dead. But he *could have* been found alive, so I rotated my hand to the right, pushing the door open.

A large fan in the waiting room blew cool air across us. Erika spied a toy car sitting on a nearby windowsill and ran to pick it up. A man came out of an office, frowned at his greasy fingers, but extended them and looked straight at me. "Hello, Mrs. Jensen, I'm Deniz, another mechanic. Come with me."

Given the emergency and the smallish repair shop, I wasn't surprised he knew who I was. I searched his face for clues about possible information. It told me nothing. I would listen and hope. The only word I couldn't accept was *dead*. I smiled at Erika scooting the car and then at Deniz. "I wonder, does the blue car have a friend?"

Deniz said, "I will find one."

He soon returned with a red car. "I'll bet this red Chevy can race the fastest," I said.

My daughter knelt on the linoleum and lined up the two cars. Deniz motioned me into the office, and I waved through the glass. I saw Erika put one hand on each roof and send the wheels spinning. The mechanic told me five men had walked the edge of the hill along several stretches.

"Did they see my son?"

Deniz dropped his head and brushed a hand through his wavy brown hair. "Someone told the police they saw an arm floating." My legs buckled. I grabbed onto a chair and fell to its seat. While I tried to slow my breathing, Deniz gave details about my husband and others searching from the road. The hillside further downriver was too rocky and steep to walk close to the water.

Erika knocked. "Mom, the red car won. Can we go now?"

I gave the toys back to Deniz and took my daughter's hand. "This nice man will take us to a guesthouse where we can stay. How about we go there and wait for your dad?"

"And Brian."

"Yes, and Brian."

Deniz walked out the door and motioned for us to follow in our car. For a short distance, the river flowed on our right, and still appeared as a swollen, sinister force. I reminded myself we were traveling upstream. Brian was downstream. Somewhere.

The road wound toward the hilltop community of Fliess. We passed knolls where white daisies danced in the breeze and Holstein cows grazed indifferently. Two days earlier at a farm stay, the kids had sat among daisies and listened to cowbells. Brian had smiled at Erika, touched every petal of one daisy, and said, "She loves me; she loves me. . . ."

The knolls and cowbells continued, and I asked my daughter, "How many cowbells can you count?"

We came to the village's narrow street with its pitched roofs and stucco buildings. Deniz pulled into a driveway. The three-story, tamarind-colored guesthouse looked solid and reassuring. I parked, and Erika said, "Eighteen cowbells."

A short but sturdy woman with a salt-and-pepper bun walked toward my open window. She wiped her eyes with a handkerchief, tucked it in her sleeve, and stretched her hands to hold mine. She said, "I Frau Mayr, Alois's mother. You family now." Her brown eyes opened wide to Erika. "You call me 'Gramma.'"

I winked at my daughter, stepped out of the car, and hugged this generous lady. Her solidness, warmth, and readiness to embrace a total stranger reminded me of Oskar's mother. Erika got out, and we three spread arms toward each other. I didn't realize how much I needed and welcomed the closeness.

Frau Mayr held Erika's hand while they walked to a door. I followed them up two flights of stairs to a hallway on the second floor. Frau stepped inside a suite and said, "You stay long as you like. No charge." We strode through the living and dining area, kitchenette, and bedroom with a king-sized bed, its comforter trimmed in tea roses. Frau told me she could bring a cot and again dabbed her eyes. I took her hand and said, "You are very kind, thank you." When Erika touched the table bouquet of edelweiss, Austria's national flower, Frau selected one flower from the vase and handed it to her.

I filled two water glasses, and my daughter finished one and poured another while I went to the balcony and took sips. The small village shops greeted me from below. Knowing I must continue to watch for signs of shock like rapid pulse and breathing in both of us, I alternated between monitoring our breathing and images of a person floating with one visible arm. I willed myself to focus on the present, take care of my daughter, and get updates about Brian.

Frau returned with a tray of apple strudel, milk, and iced tea. She smoothed her apron and hugged me. "You ask, I help you." Her compassion inspired me to carry on with hope.

I managed to taste the pastry and drink a little of the tea. Erika sat down at the table, cut a section of strudel, and set it on her tea-rose plate. She ate a small portion and drank a glass of milk. When she had swallowed the last crumb and wiped her mouth with the linen napkin, I gave her a thumbs-up. Her appetite seemed to be intact. So far, from outward signs, the tragedy hadn't appeared to overwhelm her. I was happy about that but knew she had feelings she couldn't or wasn't ready to put into words.

She went to the window that faced the back property and said, "Mom, there are apple trees." I scanned the two rows and the ground. "How about we pick up the fallen ones for more strudel?" The afternoon had become even warmer, and I sponged her face before we headed up the short hill to the orchard. There were a dozen trees, and most appeared to be a variety I knew as Irish Peach, a large apple with a pink tinge. We filled Erika's pack until the canvas bulged, and she sat down to count. "Six with brown spots and twenty with no spots." Another apple dropped close by. She jumped up, grabbed it, and sat down. "I think Dad found Brian."

My hands shook as I held them to my daughter's cheeks and kissed her. "Wherever Brian is, he knows we love him and are trying our hardest to get to him."

About six o'clock, while stretched out in the grassy orchard, we heard car doors close in the parking lot below. Oskar and Alois walked toward the guesthouse, their voices muted.

Erika ran down the hill and leaped into her father's arms. "Dad, did you find him?"

My husband's empty, sallow face had wrinkles I had never noticed, and his frame was hunched. His tense body hugged his daughter, and he shook his head. "Not yet."

An hour later, the orange sun reached toward the blue mountains, and Frau knocked softly. Oskar managed a slight smile as he shook her hand and picked up the tray from the hall table with Wiener schnitzel and potato and beetroot salads, all attractively displayed. Frau carried a chocolate cake with an American flag and held it out to Erika. "This special for you."

I walked toward my new friend, repeating, "*Danke schön, danke schön*," grasped her arms, and couldn't let go. After a few moments, I kissed her cheek, and she bowed and left. A part of me wished I had invited her to stay, her empathy filling an immediate, deep need for companionship. But I sensed Oskar would be uncomfortable, and I didn't know how Frau would feel. The sound of her feet faded, and I touched the stack of plates.

There were four dinner plates, and I held the stack for what seemed like minutes. Oskar sat down, put his elbows on the table, and bowed his head into his hands. Erika looked back and forth between her father and me, took a plate, and said, "This is for Brian," setting it in front of the fourth chair.

We joined hands, and I prayed. "Dear God, Erika, Oskar, and I are grateful beyond words to be safe. Please stay with Brian until we find him."

Embracing us through His loving arms, God ached for us. He liked joyful outcomes as much as humans . . . The question now was where to go from here. More prayer? More searching?

I chewed bites from each dish, the savory flavors and seasonings reminding me Frau had prepared this food with love. It tasted of her tenderness. Oskar silently ate a small helping of both salads and the veal and then stared at his hands. Erika scraped the vinegar-infused onions away from her potatoes and forked two bites. She swallowed a piece of veal with its crusty breading, then took a large chunk of cake with extra frosting. I cut a small slice for myself and mouthed, "Yummy," while she licked her fingers.

After Erika's last bite, she went to touch her brother's suitcase at the closet door and pulled on her bottom lip. "Why isn't Brian calling us?"

I picked up my napkin, twisted it into a rope, and blinked at Oskar. He cleared his throat, and his eyes met mine, but he said nothing. I went to scoop my daughter close. "We don't know, love, but we have to believe he's safe."

My husband stood. "I'll get the maps." He returned and opened a detailed one of the area, moving his hands over the surface and marking dots along the river. Amid copious notetaking, his furrowed brow told me not to ask questions.

The hot evening cooled a bit, and a breeze blew Erika's hair. She wiggled away from me and asked to take a bath. When I turned on the tub faucet, the flow gushed full force, and I ran out to the balcony, the river's rise continuing to unnerve me. I took several long breaths and thought about the sweetness of the apples, the cake, and Erika's ability to embrace all of it in spite of the tragedy. When she signaled that the tub was almost full, I steeled myself to go in and turn off the tap. In the steamy quiet, a slight fragrance of Irish Peach drifted through the window, and I let the aroma soak deep.

After my fingers tested the water, I helped my daughter step in. She plopped down with a splash and relaxed in the perfect temperature, rubbing a washcloth across her face. I knelt and sluiced water over her back, pushing away images of floodgates opening wide and two small children struggling to get to safety. I replayed the scene, and they were both rescued.

With Erika dry and in pajamas, I turned down the comforter, sat on the bed, and held her. Our cheeks touched as we breathed and swayed together, the tiny fragments of normalcy calming: a regular kind of dinner, a bath, snuggling, and Oskar studying maps and brochures. I challenged myself to be reassured by the prospect of a night in the clean, comfortable bed and the promise of early morning coffee. Somehow, the glass had to feel half full.

Erika didn't want a story, and I understood when she said, "I want to say my every night prayer." This night wasn't like every night, but no amount of prayer was too much to help us cope with whatever might transpire in the times ahead. We knelt beside the bed, and Oskar bent next to his daughter. Erika folded her hands under her chin. "Thank you for Mom. Thank you for Dad. Thank you for Brian. Thank you for me."

Whatever happened in the coming hours and days, I wanted us to smile at our individual ways of holding a fork, laugh at washing or not washing our faces, and applaud the kinds of compliments we gave each other. Normal steadiness had to be part of survival. I knew it would not be easy to connect with the happy parts of our lives if we didn't find Brian alive, and I counted on God giving us strength to pull through.

None of us moved until Erika spotted Rocky, her brother's stuffed bear, sitting on the comforter. Oskar must have found him in the car. She stood, picked him up along with her own Doggie, and climbed to the middle of the bed. Tucking Rocky under her left arm and Doggie under her right, I settled close beside her. Oskar stretched out next to Doggie. Three times, I reached to wind the bear's music box to honor Brian's nightly melodic message from his friend. Every time, I drew back. Finally, Erika asked her dad for the Rock-a-bye song, and Oskar turned the key. She closed her eyes. In the darkness, I wondered where Brian was. I prayed that the music was reaching him and that the soothing sounds kept him with us.

∽

With our daughter asleep, I inched to the edge of the mattress, stood, and stepped out onto the balcony. I whispered, "God, I'm here, we're here." That's all I could manage, but I did feel His closeness. Oskar silently joined me, and we watched the peaks fade into the darkening sky. Three people strolled in the street below while my husband rubbed his eyes. I slid my arm around his back. "We are all doing everything we can," I said.

He shook his head, pressed his lips tight, and closed his eyes. I rubbed his shoulder and said, "And it won't help to blame ourselves or anyone. We need to focus on the search."

"No one here thinks Brian could have survived," he said.

"But do we say he's—*dead*?" The word seemed to wail across the breeze.

The water had stayed high and fast throughout the afternoon

while Oskar and the other men scrambled over brush along the top of the incline and peered through police binoculars at rocks, root balls, and bits of debris up and down the river. Then they trekked upward through the rise and along the road. Nothing.

I wiped sweat from my forehead and folded my shaking arms. "Can't we just say we haven't found him *yet*? I don't think Erika is ready to believe Brian is dead. I'm not, either."

My husband bent his torso toward the railing. "Yes, we should say we're still looking."

I brought up calling our families. Oskar stared into the darkness and nodded, agreeing that we had to inform them. We decided his mother in Norway should take the next flight to Innsbruck while my mother should stay in Seattle, keeping the circle small. Other family and friends could send prayers and energy. Our minds needed to be clear to process the events of each day and, if Brian was dead, the opportunity to grieve privately. I clung to the one thought: *We're still looking.* Every possible rock, log, and piece of brush had to be examined before my heart could accept Brian's death. I prayed for fortitude—for Erika and Oskar and for myself.

It was midnight when we walked quietly back inside the bedroom. Oskar kept his arms down when I hugged him and softly said, "You are the hero. You saved our daughter." He strode to the right side of the bed, lay down, and pulled the covers to his forehead.

I stretched out on my side and took steps to relax into dreaming, eventually finding myself on a cushion of grass in a lush meadow, daisies popping up around me.

THREE
ELUSIVE WATER

I was jolted awake by the memory of Brian hurtling through the air. The sensation of a frozen stick pricking my spine made me shift in agony. I changed my soaked pajamas and went to the balcony for yoga poses, continuing deep breaths into the coming first light.

Images of my son's lone suitcase beside the closet door returned, and I went to stand next to it. I ran my fingers over the finely formed letters of the name tag, BRIAN S. JENSEN, and remembered how my little boy had taken such care to pack his colored pencil box, stowing it inside a sock wrapped in two shirts. The precious memory of care was paired with remorse. If we hadn't decided to picnic by the water. . . .

At 6:30 a.m., I heard clinking sounds outside the suite and discovered two hot pots and a bun warmer on a small hallway table. Frau had set them there. I carried the tray inside, poured coffee, and returned to the balcony, draping a blanket around my shoulders. I sipped the soothing brew and poured more.

At seven o'clock, Oskar padded across the wooden floor and came outside, carrying his full cup and a plate of scones. He told me two neighbors would join him for an eight o'clock riverbed search. There was a possible floodgate opening later. I wondered if he remotely considered a miraculous survival like I did.

I couldn't dismiss the feeling Brian was calling me to come

to him. "I want so much to go with you," I said. I had considered asking Frau to watch Erika but knew this request could make her uncomfortable.

My husband chewed and chewed his bite of scone. Then he was silent. Finally, he said, "You have to stay with Erika." He understood the need for normal, caring moments. And he was right. My place for now was with my daughter. Others were more suited for the river search.

Light fell on Erika's face as she stood in the open door holding an empty cup. Rocky Bear dangled from her other hand. Oskar poured hot chocolate, and she climbed onto my lap. I wrapped the blanket around her, and she drank. I said that after lunch, we would drive to Innsbruck to pick up Grandma Jensen. "Bestemor is coming!" she said, jumping to the floor.

Oskar folded the rest of his scone into a napkin, stuffed it into a pocket, and moved his face near his daughter's. "She is. Take care of Rocky and Doggie until I get back. I'm going to look for Brian." Erika's face was pensive before she dropped her bottom lip, stared at her father, and pushed Rocky Bear hard against her cheek.

Frau's voice and the fragrant breakfast aroma sent us to the table while I worked to quell the sharpening heartache. She pretended to feed the bear spoonfuls of the muesli and scrambled eggs, scooping some for herself. Her game of pretending gave me hope she was doing her best to cope—one spoonful at a time.

Minutes later, with a banana in hand, Erika ran to Brian's suitcase, opened it, and pulled his packet of pencils from the sock, lifting out and studying the blue one. Then she turned the green, yellow, and brown colors round and round.

I smiled at her as she set the sketchpad and pencils on the table and knelt on a chair, whispering, "Brian likes these colors best." I finished my small breakfast, patted her shoulder as she drew lines and images, and straightened our belongings.

The nearby homes with red and pink hanging geranium baskets, the grassy pastures, and the slate-gray hills drew me outside again. When the sight of children chasing each other across the fields became too painful, I went back to fluffing sofa pillows and listing tasks.

Erika placed her picture on my lap. She had formed a blue wavy line across the upper part of the paper with short waves underneath. Two standing figures stood near little rocks close to the bottom. A green tree and a yellow flower were nearby. "Brian and I are collecting pretty rocks away from the water." The images seemed to express her feelings.

I said, "You and Brian find treasures no one else can." She set the drawing on her father's travel log at the table and scooted onto my lap.

Could I ever describe a rock as *pretty* again? I didn't know.

Waiting for Oskar's return became more nerve-racking by the minute. Sensing Erika also needed to move and be distracted, I said, "Let's see if Frau has a ball for us to play catch in the orchard." We tossed a medium-sized one back and forth, chased it before it rolled to the street, and finally pressed it between us while we sat panting on the grass.

Oskar returned late in the morning, his eyes sunken and his demeanor an attempt to appear businesslike. He didn't need to tell me the river had risen again. Standing at the table, he studied a blank wall, then glanced at Erika's picture. She ran to pick up the drawing, and when she told her dad the story, he brightened a bit and said, "You and Brian look happy."

When Erika started another drawing, we went to the balcony, where he told me the three men had combed the river's midstream and edges for two hundred feet downriver from the accident site. They'd pulled branches and debris aside and scanned the dry bank. Forced to climb up to the hillside when the large flow returned, the group had swept away more limbs and vines. "We probed for anything, even for a shoe or shirt. Nothing." I admired my husband's courage to be back in that water so soon and to comb a hillside with almost no chance of finding evidence of Brian. I could feel how painful it was to explain the scene to me.

I still wanted to hope, but the dreadful surge stood between me and the thought of rescue.

In the afternoon, we brought Oskar's mother to the guesthouse, and Frau and Erika helped her settle into the room next to us.

When I agreed to have my mother-in-law come, I knew I had to self-talk my way through another person, even one I loved very much, being part of the unfolding drama. I vowed to embrace her caring nature.

Fortunately, Bestemor, whose real name is Hedvig, and Frau were about the same age and filled with a similar compassionate spirit. They formed an instant bond. That evening, when Frau brought dinner, Bestemor complimented her on the aromas that rose from the finely cooked food. The four of us sat down, I passed out the plates, and we joined hands. Erika and I each offered part of the thank you to God for being with us, for Bestemor's safe arrival, and for the hope of finding Brian.

My mother-in-law took a small helping of everything and praised the boiled tri-tip beef, or Tafelspitz, the sweetness of the carrots, and the crispness of the roasted potatoes. She understood well-prepared fare. Bestemor created every one of her meals with a professional

cook's experience—and much affection. Her affirmations helped my
appetite, and I saw Erika and Oskar take extra bites.

One meal, one step at a time—together. I didn't know how long
I could stay composed around another person, but I began to understand how much I needed a perspective outside my own, especially
that of a family member and a woman. I was grateful for this petite
lady with her tight, graying curls and big heart, known for expressing
herself in a gentle but straightforward manner.

At Erika's bedtime, her grandmother nestled beside her and
asked if the two of them could eat a special breakfast together in the
morning. "Can you make Norwegian soft cake?" Erika asked before
drifting into sleep.

Bestemor and I tiptoed to the balcony. I thanked her for offering
to spend time with her granddaughter so I could look for Brian. My
heart now clearly told me I needed to be part of the search, and when
Oskar joined us, I listened carefully to the details. At seven o'clock,
counting on an early small stream, he and the two neighbors would
attempt a thorough water probe past yesterday's two-hundred-foot
mark, as far as they could get.

"I'm going with you. We're in this together," I said.

June 22, 6:00 a.m.
After coffee and a Danish, we headed out. At the repair shop parking
lot, I folded my hands and asked for several hours of low water.

The four of us tramped to the edge of the hillside to peer at the
area where the group stopped searching yesterday. I stared at the
slow, narrow water. Our binoculars focused; we looked downriver
and then climbed the incline to the rocks. Pausing at sticks and logs
both in and out of the water, we carefully stepped around medium

and large jagged boulders. Nothing. When the boulders became close and too rugged to navigate, we climbed back to the ridge and inspected the area with binoculars. I stopped every few minutes to listen for rolling and sloshing, but standing far above the water, I wondered why. When the hill became too vertical to peer under vegetation and lift blackberry vines, we walked along the road.

I found it disheartening that there was no trace of my son. Still, I couldn't give up the image of him, conscious or unconscious, trapped under a log or lying deep in the brush, my mind stretching his survival time beyond anything realistic. At eleven thirty, I asked the two men the question I had been avoiding: "Do you think there's even a one percent chance Brian is alive?"

Each man dropped his head. Part of me said I should believe them, but the other part felt helpless to do so.

I drove back to the guesthouse to be with my daughter. From the doorway, I watched her kneeling behind the sofa, holding wild daisies. Finally, she noticed me and crawled out. "See, Mom, I found all the flowers Grandma hid. We picked them in the orchard."

I took the bouquet and said, "Let's get them a drink." I found a vase and water and set the container on the lamp table.

Erika opened her brother's sketchpad to a new page. "I'm going to draw Brian and me picking daisies on a hillside, like we did at that farm," she said.

Bestemor saw that I wanted to talk and followed me to the balcony. We stood at the railing, and she took my hand in the warming morning. "Sometimes mothers feel things fathers don't."

I threw my arms around her and, through sobs, said, "When does a mother give up hope of finding her son alive?"

"Janice, you know your precious Brian better than anyone. Your heart will tell you what to believe. And you have faith in the Eternal."

I understood she believed our reunion would not be on this earth.

This was the third day. It was unlikely Brian would be alive, even if he had been thrown out of the water. Exposure and lack of medical attention would almost certainly have caused him to die.

I spread peanut butter on a slice of bread, and Erika arranged banana pieces and then pressed more bread on top. She took a bite as Oskar walked in the door at one o'clock, his steps deliberate, his countenance pale. She jumped to the floor, ran to her father, and lifted her arms. He held her close while shaking his head several times. Bestemor stopped pouring apple juice and wiped a tear. I almost dropped the serving bowl of Frau's dumpling soup. Finally, I dished a spoonful and said, "How about we check out the recreation center this afternoon? Maybe they'll have Crazy Eights and Go Fish and balls to throw." I high-fived my daughter, knowing she loved games of all kinds.

Erika slipped her untouched carrot sticks to her grandmother's plate and said, "Remember when Brian and I won every game on Christmas Eve?" I thought about how, as I had turned out the lights at midnight, inches of snow piled up on our trees and walkway. Bestemor said, "Yes, over three snowy days, we played every card and board game in your house." After she had swallowed her last bite of sandwich, Erika asked to be excused to put on shorts.

Oskar and I stayed at the table while he told me about the late-morning efforts at the river. He and the two men looked from the road and heard the deluge return. The Inn River veers left at the west edge of Landeck, three miles north of Nesselgarten, where it meets the Sanna River, becoming very wide. They talked about expanding the search at that juncture but decided the conditions wouldn't allow them to find a child without the help of a skilled rescue team. None existed for hire or as volunteers. I said, "At least we know what won't happen."

We set out for the recreation center in the early afternoon, motoring through the village and for two miles along a narrow gravel road. Barns and hay wagons sat scattered on both sides. Soon an off-white rectangular building appeared on the right. The sign at the top read FLIESS SWIM CENTER. I didn't remember being told the recreation center had a pool.

Oskar parked, and Bestemor offered to see if they had games to play. Through my closed car window, I watched children and parents come out the door, laughing and shouting. I wiped my flushed cheeks and runny nose. Erika leaned forward, "Mom, are you okay?" It turned out the center had no games, so my daughter and her grandmother decided to count barns and cows on the hillsides. I was glad to leave the pool behind.

On the return trip, when we again passed the swim center, something made me blurt out, "Please pull into the parking lot." I rolled down my window to see a teenage girl run through the front door, giggling. A man's voice drifted out from behind the chain-link fence at the right, and I caught the German word for "catch," *fangen*. No one moved until Erika opened her door, studied the fence, and tapped my arm. We got out, and she took my hand and led me across the asphalt. Midway, she brushed hair from her eyes and squinted at two girls at the shallow end. Soon, her face was pressed against the fence.

The girls, about her age, blew bubbles into the water and tossed and caught an orange ball with an instructor. I saw them hold their "puffs" while Erika mimicked the action. After a few minutes, the two came through the front door, and my daughter smiled at them. We held hands, and she skipped to the car.

Blowing bubbles evoked images of the water Brian must have coughed out when he was washed away, and of me inhaling and swallowing water when I tried to learn to swim. My shoulders stiffened.

But all the way to the guesthouse, I thought, *Okay, I stood at the river and near deep water at the pool today. Even with the frightening river memories, I can go in the slow, narrow stream behind the service center and confirm there is no trace of Brian. By myself and for myself. I will have searched every possible rock and turned over every branch that could lodge him. My heart can catch up with my mind.*

Dinner was finished, the table cleared, and Erika tucked in. Oskar opened his travel book and logged expenses. I pulled my chair close and told him my plan. He dropped his jaw and asked why. I took his hands and said, "Because then my heart can be settled that Brian was beyond reach," adding I would wear a life vest, go in slow water no higher than my calves, and carry a walking stick. He shook his head and went outside to the car. An hour later, he returned and looked at me, with lips forming a straight line across his face, cheeks tight, and unblinking eyes. This told me he had concluded Brian was beyond the ability to be found.

While I respected his position, I needed proof through my own rendezvous.

Lake Meridian, south of Seattle, June 1946: I was seven years old. My friend Cindy took my hand and pulled me into water up to my knees. I grabbed her bathing suit and tugged on her arm. When small waves almost knocked me down, I yanked my hands away in panic and splashed quickly to shore. It was a breezy Sunday afternoon at her family's picnic, and Cindy's father, standing nearby, asked if I was okay. I nodded and watched him lift his daughter and toss her deeper. She dog-paddled right back to him as if she had done it a hundred times. I decided water activities were not fun. And I soon realized why.

Two weeks later at the same beach, Cindy crawled out of the back seat of our car and called, "Come on, Janice." My mom had signed us up for beginner swim lessons. I stood beside the open door, hugging the cardigan I'd buttoned over my swimsuit while my friend ran to join the group of children.

Finally, I waded into the shallow lake and held Cindy's hand—tighter every step—until we stood in water up to our knees. When teacher Jenny said, "Drop your arms and splash your face," the waves pushed against my thighs, and I started to slip, grabbing the bathing suit ruffle of the girl on my right. When the water was at our waist, I dug my fingernails into Cindy's palm. She yelled, "Ouch," and tugged her hand away.

During those eight weeks, my skinny body shivered every time I had to bring my face to the water. A flood gushed up my nose, and I lifted my head, coughing and spitting. When I stretched out to float and kick, I held my breath, ran out of air, and sank. As a young adult, I took private lessons and practiced the crawl, the breaststroke, and treading water. I never learned to swim well enough to save myself.

All my efforts only reinforced what my body had told me at a young age. I lacked buoyancy—a swim-worthy body. My desire to learn became a cause to support others. Brian and Erika favored their father's build and ability to float. As their mother, I did want my children to respect and enjoy the water and to be good swimmers. Oskar's successful effort to push against the current and save his daughter is a testament to his strength and skill. I would always champion that determination and ability.

FOUR
DETERMINATION AND PURPOSE

June 23, 5:30 a.m.

Y most courageous self would wade into the same river that
sent my son plunging downstream.

I crept out of bed, dressed in the bathroom, and stowed binoculars and a thermos of hot tea in my pack. With no other cars on the road, I opened the windows and took in the solitude. At the top of the hill behind the service center, I pictured finding a scrap of Brian's clothing, and it stopped me. How would I feel if I actually saw his shirt or a fragment of it? Remembering my purpose—to leave no stone unturned—I pushed onward.

Long strides took me down the trail, treading on the roots and stepping over the rocks. The same sleepy eel of a flow greeted me as when we had come to explore and picnic. My life vest fastened, I checked for the whistle in my pocket and paced through the stones, their scraping sounds familiar.

I will put my drowning fears aside. If they appear, I will send them away and pray they don't return.

Through the binoculars, I scanned the river far and wide. With lenses adjusted for distance, I peered at both shorelines and slopes downriver as far as detail allowed. Nothing hinted that a small boy had been there. Walking stick planted firmly and light green, algae-covered rocks clear in the slow flow, I stepped inch by inch forward and sideways through the slippery water from Brian's rock downstream. I veered to the dry area on both sides. The quiet flow gently splashed at my calves and wet the full-length travel pants I had tucked into the borrowed boots. I bent until my back ached, stood up, and crouched again. The snowmelt-cold river sent chills up my spine and began to numb my feet in their wool socks. I dropped the thermos cup while drinking the last of the tea, fingers stiff from pulling away leaves and small plants.

When I came to the boulders and large rocks too dangerous to navigate, I stood still, not wanting to give up the river search. My mind had told me Brian wasn't in that part of the long flow, and this minute, my heart had caught up. Finally, I climbed up the embankment, my slippery footwear distracting me from the sadness of not finding any evidence of my son. A shoe or a piece of his blue shirt would not have signaled survival, but it would have been one more reminder of his bravery.

Inspecting jagged rocks and separating tangled limbs in the cold water gave me permission to release Brian's body to the elements. I had turned over every possible stone. The act let me view my son in an altruistic way: he was dead, but his strong character would live on.

Without thought or reason, I lifted bushes and branches all the way to the top of the hill. Keeping Brian in the forefront of my mind had become automatic. I was startled to see Alois walking toward me. We hugged, and he told me he had been watching and was coming to help. Nodding, he said, "I'm glad you searched. You loved your son, and he loved you like only a mother and son can. My mother and I love the same way."

It was nine o'clock when I changed into dry clothes and drove back to the guesthouse. Leaning against a tree in the orchard, I touched a low-hanging apple. The fruit was redolent with fragrance and beauty, telling me life would go on. And with purpose. The best I could do was find my truth and embrace the paths I was meant to travel.

No one was up when I opened the door to the suite, poured coffee, and sat on the balcony. Soon, Oskar came out with his cup, steam swirling across his face. He blinked and looked toward the distant mountains. I faced the direction of the river and closed my eyes. We were silent together.

In a few minutes, loud voices inside the suite startled us. Erika and Bestemor cleaned up orange juice that had spilled across the white tablecloth. When we sat down to breakfast, Erika said, "Mom, can we go to the pool today?" Her enthusiasm yesterday meant she likely would ask to go again. We both put on shorts and T-shirts; Bestemor wore a dress and carried a sun hat. Oskar dropped us off at the edge of the parking lot on his way to Landeck. It was ten o'clock and already in the low eighties.

Again, my daughter took my arm, but this time, we walked to the front door, and she opened it. With permission from the lobby desk and before I could change my mind, I turned the knob to open the gate to the pool. Erika faced the large rectangle and rubbed her eyes, a familiar gesture when she was weighing her options. I smoothed my hand across her back as I took in the sight of kids bouncing and playing ball tag below sunny skies. One of the girls from yesterday saw my daughter and threw a ball toward her. It landed near the fence. Erika ran to pick it up, held it, then tossed it back. Several more tosses came and went; each time, the ball landed closer between the two girls.

Bestemor clapped from the only chair while I leaned against the fence. The gestures and expressions told her the girls were having fun. At first, when I heard loud splashes, I turned to face the parking lot. After telling myself, *You are meant to welcome this fun,* I girded myself and waved at the ball going back and forth.

In a few minutes, the instructor from yesterday left the lifeguard platform and went inside. I followed him, and he introduced himself as Rudolf. Briefly describing Erika's recent trauma, I found out he knew most of the details. He said he believed she was handling being around water well and wanted to invite her to join his class, where Hannah and Marie were learning to float. "It might help her to know that."

I shared how Erika had been comfortable at home in Oregon with her face in water, and could float, kick, and do a rudimentary crawl, but I wasn't sure what to expect from her now. Rudolf came poolside with me, sat at the edge, and smiled at my daughter standing nearby. "Those are cool shorts, and I'll bet you don't care if they get a little wet," he said. Her look seemed to puzzle him, but he stood, picked up a ball, and said, "Would you like to hold my hand and walk down one step?"

Erika reached for Rudolf, and soon, water lapped at her feet on the third step. She threw the ball a short distance, and someone threw it back. Then the instructor said, "Can I toss one to you from the bottom?" She nodded. After three back-and-forth tosses, other kids came to grab the ball. Every time Erika pitched it back, Bestemor said, "Good throw."

Then without warning, she dropped her arms and came to me. "Let's go, Mom."

Rudolf caught up with us at the gate. "See you tomorrow, Erika?" he said.

She looked at the pool and at the smiling instructor, wiped her cheeks, and timidly nodded. In the taxi, while she settled close, I said it was up to her if she went back, and that we could talk about it.

I had to poke the key into the lock at the guesthouse three times before I could position it to open the door. My distress at facing the river so intimately earlier had caught up with me, along with the image of almost losing both Erika and Oskar. Bestemor took Erika for a walk through the village to count geranium baskets.

I ran to the bedroom, locked the door, and let the sobs come.

June 24, 1972

The morning of day five, I woke early thinking about logistics, such as when we should leave, and a possible celebration of Brian's life here in Austria. We had approved a plan for Oskar's company office in Innsbruck to plant a tree in Brian's memory on their property near the river and to install a bench and plaque.

Erika tapped my shoulder at eight and whispered, "Mom, can I go and play ball with the girls at the swimming pool?" Rubbing my eyes, I nodded and glanced at Oskar, who had asked to sleep late.

Before ten o'clock, Erika, wearing her swimsuit under her clothes, sat with Bestemor in the back seat as I drove the two miles to the pool. As we walked to the steps at the shallow end, Rudolf stretched out his arms, and my daughter pulled off her shirt and shorts. "Glad you came, Erika. Come down to my hands," he said. He led her to the pool floor, where she smiled at Hannah and Marie and joined them in blowing bubbles. *I will trust my Erika with Rudolf.*

I sat on the cement, four feet from the edge, and took shallow breaths. The instructor told the three girls if they floated and blew bubbles, he would reward them with a game of ball toss. First, he supported Erika from both sides, then lightly under her middle. On her first try alone, she held her head back and started to sink. But soon, she kicked across the pool, inhaled to her left and right, and blew bubbles into the water. After a last bubble, she stood, snorted, and wiped her nose. I knelt close to her and clapped like she had won a medal while Bestemor cheered, *Hurrah!* over and over. A message of courage and boldness I could build on—even if I would never be a real swimmer.

It was almost one o'clock when Erika was ready to leave. Embracing Rudolf at the door, I said, "Thank you for treating my daughter like every other child."

Back at the guesthouse, she burst into the room and threw her arms around Oskar's waist, her face against his shirt. "I swam in the pool today!" she said.

He picked her up and said with a grin I hadn't seen since before the accident, "Good for you. You are so brave." He added quietly, "Braver than I am."

Shoulder to shoulder with my husband, I whispered, "You are both valiant!"

Erika sat at the table with a piece of my notebook paper and felt pens, drawing herself and Brian paddling a canoe, a large image of me at the shore waving hello.

Later, I said to Oskar, "Please believe you are not responsible for Brian's drowning. The power company is. You have to believe that."

I had to keep giving myself the same message.

FIVE
A SIGN, GOODBYE, AND BONDING

L unch was a victory celebration for Erika. Red, yellow, and green sprinkles melted into a rainbow of color on her vanilla ice cream. My daughter's sweet success filled me.

Aware that the Inn River's fury came without a hint of warning, I kept returning to the subject of signs. I was certain none existed behind the service center along the trail to the water, nor in the extended woods where we searched for Brian. Maybe one was buried under vegetation along the road farther east leading to the repair shop. If I did a check and found one, I could confirm that the government had made a small attempt at some point to keep the public safe.

Oskar and I walked the roadside that afternoon downriver for two miles toward Landeck. We probed under all the greenery possible for a scrap and found zero notices. The following day, our quest focused on possible buried fragments on the hillside behind the service center and downstream. We dug deeper under half-dead pieces of wood than our search for Brian had taken us and yanked at mixtures of stickers and debris. Oskar peeled back layers of anything that looked propitious. Not a single scrap of metal or wooden post surfaced.

At three o'clock in the humid air, some fifty feet upstream from a rudimentary path and near a stretch of road we hadn't traveled, I pushed my wobbly legs across fallen branches and vines. Each step felt more pointless. *Just a few more feet before it's time to leave.*

My right foot caught on woody vegetation, and I lurched forward. Oskar grabbed my arm while my left shoe landed on a hard surface. With bare hands, I jerked away creepers and brush. Eight by ten inches of rusty metal lay at my feet, loosely attached to a scrap of wood. Parts of words remained on the bullet-riddled fragment, and I pieced together the message: *Achtung, Wasserschwall.* (Caution, Floodwater.) Kneeling, I touched the jagged metal. It was an ominous token of a warning that should have been intact, fully visible in English, French, and German, and replicated throughout the area.

In the 1970s, it appeared European countries like Austria had tough river and mountaineering regulations for rafters and climbers, but apparently not for the viewing public. Still on my knees, I confronted this lack of concern, censuring those charged with keeping the public safe. Oskar walked around the rusty piece again and again, shaking his head. Inside the car, he started the engine and, without looking at me, said, "Let's go."

Back at the guesthouse, Erika greeted us with a paper bird she and Bestemor had made and colored with the orange, black, and green pencils. "We watched birds fly in the orchard, and then I made my own," she said. When I told her it looked like a chaffinch, she flew it across the room, her cheeks sporting the same orange color. When the bird landed behind a chair, she sat down to make another one and then held the two noses together.

The next morning, Erika polished off Frau's special scrambled eggs, swung her legs back and forth, and said to her father, "You have to watch me swim across the pool."

I gave her a high five while telling Oskar she remembered everything she had learned at home.

We stopped at the swim center on our way to Innsbruck. Erika
took her father's hand and led him to the poolside chair, while
Bestemor stood beside him. Our daughter smiled at each of us and
walked into the water to her waist. With Rudolf nearby, she extended
her arms, breathed in at a side, and pushed her body forward with
strong kicks. She even pulled her arms back for a couple of crawl
strokes. After steadying herself at the wall and wiping her eyes, she
said to her father, "Did you see my bubbles?"

Oskar knelt in front of her. "I saw a girl who likes to swim," he
said.

Unspoken sentiment told us it was time to go home and rebuild togetherness. As a family of three. That afternoon, before taking Bestemor
to the airport, we went to Oskar's company office for Brian's short
memorial. The Norway maple had been planted in a small garden
where breezes from the river sent branches and leaves dancing. The
cedar bench, which also faced the water, included a brass strip with
BRIAN S. JENSEN in large italics. We listened to a prayer given by
the branch manager and heard "Morning Has Broken," sung by an
employee accompanying himself on a guitar.

At our airport goodbyes to Bestemor, Erika wrapped her arms
around her grandmother. "Come and watch me swim laps." My
mother-in-law told her she would visit and to keep practicing. Then
she pulled Oskar and me close.

"You'll see Brian again," she said.

I folded my arms around her and affirmed that she had blessed
us with love like none other.

She embraced her son. He simply said, "Thank you, Mor."

After dinner at the guesthouse, Erika crawled onto my lap with Rocky and Doggie. She played the bear's Rock-a-bye song and pressed her head to my chest. "I want to bring Brian home and bury him by the maple tree with two trunks." The tree was her brother's favorite in our woods.

I rocked her and told her we couldn't do that because we didn't find him. "God knows exactly where he is and will take care of him," I said. She climbed down to set Doggie on a chair, crawled onto the bed, and curled up with Rocky. She prayed for Brian, her dad, me, and herself, for Bestemor, and for her brother's bear.

June 27, Early morning

Oskar readied the car for travel again and the drive to Amsterdam, where it would be shipped to Oregon. I walked through the suite collecting our belongings and picked up my sweater from the sofa. I smoothed its cushions, remembering how this solid structure had supported me when I sat to gather courage.

My finger circled the rim of the rose-painted teacup that Frau had given me, saying, "Fill it with love." I wrapped the porcelain carefully and stood one last time on the cooling balcony.

Frau brought a savory cheese quiche and cranberry muffins dotted with sparkling sugar crystals and accepted our invitation to eat this final meal with us. I cut a piece of quiche, forked a bite, and savored the flavors while the muffin's bouquet lingered. Each sensation had the assurance of a heartfelt remembrance.

The room was silent until Frau spoke. "I don't have daughter, granddaughter, or son-in-law. You always be mine." Oskar blinked, opened and closed his mouth, and tried to say something. I knew he treasured being Frau's honorary son-in-law.

We had to face the anguish of leaving Brian behind in a gravesite far away, known only as the Inn River. This generous woman and her kind son had challenged us to think beyond grief. They stood for bringing all of life together and finding hidden gems of happiness. Frau and I embraced, cheek to cheek, and I said, "You and Alois fill our hearts with promise."

Oskar stood and took the last two suitcases to the car. When he came back to pick up his camera and travel log, Erika clutched her brother's bear and said, "Rocky and I are going home to climb Brian's favorite tree with Sunny." Sunny was her brother's cat.

The idea of a home without our son seemed to freeze Oskar at the doorway. He eyed the suite as if unfamiliar and hurried out the door, empty-handed.

We stopped at the service center to give Alois one last embrace of gratitude.

As we left Nesselgarten, I watched a few streaks of sun glint through thick, dark clouds, a reminder that light shines through darkness.

I turned to check on Erika as we drove toward Landeck. She looked up from her brochure about Tivoli Gardens, the second oldest amusement park in the world, then stretched to tap her father's shoulder. "Dad, when will we get to the roller coaster?" Before we left Oregon, Oskar had promised our children a trip to Copenhagen, and when he asked Erika yesterday if she still wanted to go, she took his hand and said, "I want to ride the roller coaster all day and night."

Three days later, she spotted this favorite ride before we entered the gate. Her father bought them all-day passes for the park's carnival thrills. "Have barrels of fun. You both deserve it," I said. Every time I checked in with them, Oskar related how much Erika shrieked on the roller coaster, always asking for more drops and twists. He admitted the rides were even better than during his youth.

If I had needed another example of the differences between experiences that gave Erika and Oskar a rush but left me trembling, it would be the rides at Tivoli. I walked beside hyacinths and flowering cherry trees and strolled along the lakes with their cascading fountains. The sights, sounds, and fragrances of nature brought a bit of peace each time I took a deep breath.

By dusk, when a rainbow of hues lit every tree, building, and mechanized feature, father and daughter had chalked up six trips on the roller coaster, and more than one on several other rides with drops, twists, and turns. Still bouncing as we relaxed on a bench near midnight, Erika said, "Can we come back tomorrow and the day after that?" Her eyes seemed to plead.

A last-minute decision saw us travel to Sandefjord, Norway, to be with Oskar's extended family and friends. His parents had retired to the coastal town where aunts, uncles, and cousins had resettled. What I remember most about the visit are the times my husband's expressions resembled those before the accident—characteristically muted but evident.

He spoke Norwegian to his cousins and friends, reminiscing about childhood and young-adult fun on the ski slopes and hikes through Europe. During those brief exchanges, I saw almost-smiles of a person trying a little openness. For short moments, he answered questions about the drowning, his words measured. After extended minutes of his cousins querying me for information, I was struggling to maintain my composure.

I was more comfortable engaging with my daughter and the children. I could speak limited Norwegian, Erika and I having taken a university class. We also spoke English while organizing hide-and-seek games, going on treasure hunts for lingonberries and wild strawberries, and writing and drawing pictures for matching words in the two languages.

After each child had drawn and cut out a Norwegian fairy tale paper doll character, a group of mothers, aunts, and grandmothers helped glue a Popsicle stick on the back of each one. Then we stood in a circle, holding puppets and singing "Frère Jacques" (Fader Jakob) to each character in English and Norwegian. The camaraderie was unexpected, but Erika and I welcomed it.

SIX

LIFE BEFORE THE INN RIVER

Oskar and I met in 1960 while completing bachelor's degrees at the University of Washington, his in mathematics, mine in liberal arts. We married in 1961, and Brian was born the following year. Our shared faith offered a spiritual structure we valued for our children, prompting us to join an affiliate congregation east of Seattle. It was led by Pastor Dan, who became a lifelong friend.

After six years as a Boeing systems engineer, my husband was hired by a company that offered a job in Western Oregon. The natural areas and extensive trails appealed to us, along with the beauty of the Willamette River and the locally based business community. Brian was six, and Erika was three when we moved into our new home. Pastor Dan and his family had also relocated to Oregon.

Thanksgiving morning, 1968, found us unloading living room and bedroom furniture. With the large pieces and some boxes settled, Brian asked if he could explore the woods. I watched my son pull his sand bucket out of a box, head down the back-deck stairs, and in a few minutes, come through the laundry room door. Hiding his bucket behind him, he whispered he had found cones with three fingers and shiny purple rocks. Presents for Erika.

One evening in early December, he held up a large tablet to his father and asked if the two could draw trails for our backwoods. They took photos of the areas with the big Doug firs, maples, and oaks, and sat together several different evenings to pencil images where the paths could wind through and around the trees. Brian drew the blackberry bushes and put an X over them. Erika took her brother's suggestion, coloring the trees with three different greens and the path a dark brown. Oskar put checkmarks beside most sections as a *go forward* sign, the sketch becoming our landscape plan.

The third week of January, we had what townsfolk called "The Big Snow." Three feet fell in less than forty-eight hours. Neighbor Tom spent a morning helping Oskar and me turn our front yard into a maze where our children and Tom's played hide-and-seek for days. Brian called out, "I can't find Erika," then feigned surprise when she jumped out at him.

We spent cold evenings that winter and the next three near our warm living room fireplace, making music with "instruments" of lids, forks, and bottles. Oskar watched the three of us the first few times, not convinced this could be fun. Finally, handed two forks by his son, who said, "Just try it," his stiff shoulders and hands melded clinks with Brian's giggles.

I settled back on the pillows of the new rust-colored sofa to read, the kids usually joining me. When I kissed their hands and gave them hugs, they often motioned to their father, who was reading in the chair he and Brian had selected, named Ocean Blue. If Oskar came, the kids squeezed us close together and snuggled on either side. They talked about how warm we felt.

I always gave my husband a hug and kiss before the two of us fell asleep. His response was often a more formal arm pat and occasionally a kiss, his introspective personality holding back more physical affection, no matter the relationship or age of the person.

Beginning with our courtship, I chose to adjust my outward shows of devotion to his more pragmatic demonstrations of love—gifts of candy, dresses, and sweaters selected for my taste, expensive kitchen gadgets I joyfully welcomed, and money to buy *whatever I wanted.* I often commented about the overpriced chocolates and the army-green outfit he called "a battle uniform" for difficult professional days. All of the gestures made life more fun.

Oskar had grown up in Oslo but spent summers on his grandparents' farm, watering pea vines and milking goats. He helped his grandfather clean the barn and organize the tools. When he had to come inside, he curled up with a book away from the clatter of indoor living.

As a child, I spent endless hours with my mother reading cookbook recipes. While we measured ingredients for a rice and hamburger casserole, I would ask if we could stir carrots into the mixture instead of onions. Mom usually smiled and told me we had to follow the recipe exactly or the dish might not taste right. Occasionally, she relaxed her strict practices, and one time, when I asked if I could spoon as much whipped cream into the fruit salad as snowy Mount Rainier, she said, "Pile it high."

My mother taught me to believe that the Written Word's spiritual dogma was simple and practical. She said it was only right to treat the people who live under a bridge with the same respect and kindness we give our friends and heroes.

My father bonded with animals, seeing both wild and tame as innocent and often deprived of their own health and safety. Once, my brother Bobby and I rescued two kittens from a garbage can and hid them in our woodshed. We snuck boiled eggs and water to them until we could pool our allowances and buy a bag of cat food. Although we already had two rescued cats and a dog, Dad finally convinced Mom the cats needed a home—ours.

On favorite streamside camping trips, Bobby and I headed to the water to watch beavers gnaw sticks, paddle them, and build dams. Dad told us that beaver shelters slow down the flow and help prevent erosion of plants and other materials. Snuggled in my sleeping bag, I dreamed how cozy the beavers must be.

Dad loved me—and everyone—without limit. And he believed that passion must be part of all learning. Every Friday night after dinner, while the turntable played the "Tennessee Waltz," we faced each other, clasped arms, and he led me in a waltz pattern of one count back and two sideways. Without a word, Dad showed me that music, body, and deep thought blended to express emotion. I loved stepping forward to meet him, usually bouncing and beaming. He never complained about my awkwardness or "two left feet."

We whirled together and counted the *quick, quick, slow* rhythm of "Don't Fence Me In." The power of bonding through movement and the expansion of a relationship through time spent together made a lasting impression. Had he lived longer than my fifteenth year, Dad and I would have danced our way through many steps, routines, and original ideas.

His greatest gift was honoring my independent thinking.

Although he would never dance a waltz, Oskar believed in the goal of sharing talents and love as a parent, professional, and friend to those who needed someone.

On a fall weekend when Brian was almost nine, we drove to Central Oregon to explore. Each of us chose a specific interest, mine being an underground cave where molten lava had stopped pouring and produced a hollow circle at the top. It seemed scary but intriguing, and Oskar offered to stay with the kids while I investigated the rocks and openings. I hadn't read details of what others had found, preferring to discover my own revelations. I put on my headlamp, a warm jacket, and proper walking shoes. Brian stood in front of me, his little face serious. "I want to come with you," he said. Although my first thought was that we could both fall or get hurt, I also saw it as an adventure. Oskar blinked a slow blink. I should take my son and only go as far as he was comfortable.

It was noon when we stepped carefully down a long ladder in low light onto a rocky landscape, our headlamps on. We zipped our jackets in the cool dampness and listened. Our coughs echoed. We trod over jagged rocks to the middle of the large cave, stood still, and gazed upward. A beam of sun began to appear through the broad, circular opening. Headlamps off, we watched the light get stronger. Brian said, "I see tiny sunbeams."

We walked a bit farther inward, where a smaller opening and beam appeared, and still deeper into the cave, where a third light shone across our faces. A thin mist rose from the damp earth and met the sun. Our headlamps off again, Brian grinned, lifted his arms, and said, "Sunbeams. Like tiny sunflowers."

We crept to the end of the tunnel, where I was sure I heard a white-nosed bat flutter, but my son reminded me they wouldn't arrive until next month.

In our family, each person belonged, found their path, and thrived.

SEVEN

FACING THE FAMILIAR

Three instead of four . . . my repeated phrase during the long plane ride home. Respite in Norway, downtime at Tivoli, and bonding with Frau and Alois helped me trust life to hold meaning and some normalcy while we processed loss and ways to cope. Brian found joy in giving to others. With time and patience, I wanted to believe each of us could experience real love of ourselves and bring joy to each other and the world.

It was mid-July, and an abundance of cottonwood, maple, and birch trees, along with acres of bean vines, met us as we approached the local airport. When we walked off the plane, Erika pulled her baseball cap tight to shade her eyes, and I lowered my broad-brimmed sun hat against the heat.

The taxi turned into our driveway in front of the lime-green, trilevel house with the towering maple. I wasn't prepared for the memory of Brian and Erika running up and down the oval-shaped lawn, blowing bubbles for Sunny cat. I scrunched my hat close as I struggled to face the present reality and stayed seated until the luggage had been unloaded.

After Oskar opened the front door, I ran up the walk and dashed inside, quickly stepping back out to grab Brian's suitcase. Sunny scurried to me and pressed between my legs. In the foyer, he purred against my calves, sniffed his master's bag, and rubbed his cheek against a corner. With my husband's tacit acceptance, I set the suitcase at the back of the hall closet.

A foyer wall held the collage of photos of our days in Seattle with our young children. I stood glancing at my favorites. One showed Brian pushing our white-footed black cat in a doll stroller. We had named him "Little Boots Jensen," and when he roamed, Brian joined me in calling, "LBJ." One of my son's delights was placing a fresh towel in a laundry room box where LBJ often slept. I touched the photo of our daughter floating flower petals in a wading pool and remembered how she blew her strongest breaths to get them to "swim." Wiping my eyes, I promised the quick looks would somehow help me cherish the past.

When I stole a glance into the living room, the tables, chairs, and lamps looked back with distress. Baby pictures by the fireplace and an album of recent family snapshots glared. I glared back at them and at the distant dining room and its shiny walnut table, where family members and friends often gathered for meals and conversation. Today the wood felt like an impostor, and the room's contents seemed to buzz with spite: *We're just wood, cloth, or metal. We can't give you happiness and hope.*

The void stabbed at my core, and I wondered if I could ever again feel that life was vital and precious. Could this house ever again herald joy? Another reality: if the furniture and accoutrements of fun from this family of four were packed up, the images, sounds, and sensibilities of our former lives would still reverberate through the walls.

It was hard to visualize the sorrowful us as a thriving family in this home. How would I feel sending one child off to school? Greet Brian's friends without him? And oh, the sympathy, the efforts people make to provide comfort. I couldn't think about it. And I hadn't found the words to ask Oskar or Erika how they felt about this house.

I closed myself to more memories, including a glance into the bedrooms on the upper level. Things like touching Brian's drawings, picking up books he and Erika read together, or smoothing the down comforter on our bed where we all snuggled on Sunday mornings were beyond my heart's reach. For now, I would pretend everything was unchanged.

On the back deck, I breathed in fresh earthy scents and closed my eyes against images of our shattered life.

When I heard Erika talk to Sunny, I looked inside and saw him jump onto the sofa and her lap. She held him, kissed each cheek, and waited for his nose to sniff hers and purr. Brian's words, *best purrer* and *smartest cat*, seemed to echo from the empty cushion. Although I had no idea what to do the next minute, I had to consider that happy words and ideas would continue to come.

Erika came out to the deck and said there was a chocolate cake on the kitchen counter. I went inside with her, thinking no one but the cat sitter had known of our arrival. Breads and a bowl of apples and bananas were nearby, and a note on a pink paper heart read, "More in the fridge. We love you. Gayle, Marlene, and Marilyn." Opening the door to the salads and entrées, I closed my eyes in thankfulness to my neighbor friends. Our families had eaten dinners together, hiked in the hills, and planted tree seedlings. Bounty had come once again. A bit of relief. Somehow, it felt as if Frau Mayr were part of these offerings.

I set the potato salad, baked beans, and vegetable tray on the back picnic table, along with watermelon slices and the chocolate cake. Erika called her dad. As I took a small bite of potato salad, I thought of the loving hands that had prepared this beautiful food, and, with some effort, I tasted and enjoyed the different offerings. Oskar appeared to be glad for the nourishment.

Our daughter tasted everything and asked to be excused before dessert. She ran to her room, returned with her Fisher Price dollhouse, and set it at the end of the table. While Oskar and I opened mail, she pulled open both sections, moved furniture and people to different rooms, and whispered to the tiny wooden doll heads. After she closed the two parts again, I said, "Your dolls must be happy you are home to take care of them."

She shook her head. "The girl doll is looking for her brother."

My mind went blank. When I let myself breathe, I held my daughter and whispered, *He has to be away now, but he'll be safe where he is.*

Erika picked up Rocky Bear beside her and went to find Sunny.

Around eight o'clock, she came downstairs in her pajamas, holding the cat. Looking into her dad's eyes, she said, "Rocky and I want to sleep with you and Mom. Can Sunny come, too?"

Oskar had never let the cat sleep in our bed, but he nodded with a look that said, *Only this once.* I followed Erika up the stairs, thankful to see that Brian's door was closed, and helped her snuggle into the middle of our California king, Rocky and Sunny beside her. The cat purred during an entire story and through the prayer when Oskar joined us.

As our daughter breathed in sleep, we slowly stood. A happy memory of the four of us telling stories while snuggled under the Norwegian down flashed to me. I touched the quilt, a gift from Bestemor, and seeing my husband's downcast eyes and pursed lips, reassured him that someday it would feel cozy again. He walked away while I savored my own tiny piece of cheer.

Oskar gathered travel books and maps and took them to his downstairs office. I watched him open one of Western Europe and trace the Inn River from its source in Switzerland. He said, "With the Swiss initiating the flow into the Austrian power grid, Austria doesn't have much control over the level and timing." He folded the map neatly to its smallest size and placed it inside a large dictionary at the back of a top shelf, then walked hurriedly out the door.

I had come to that same conclusion during the days we looked for Brian. The giant power company's agenda was beyond us, and it was time to put our questions about their culpability out of mind.

Later, standing in our bedroom, I put my forehead against my husband's and said, "I'm grateful that in our neighborhood, we hear only the sounds of trees, crickets, and wind." He faintly smiled, and we slid into bed, our daughter between us. I reached across the sheets to find Oskar's hand and pressed it.

At sunup, I heard kitchen cupboards opening and closing and found Erika, still wearing her pajamas, sitting on the carpet of the lower-level family room. A bowl of Cheerios rested on her lap. Her dollhouse was open wide, and two tiny figures sat on chairs beside a table while she lifted a girl child to another chair. She fed them all Cheerios and said, "The mom and dad and sister are hungry."

With my arm around my daughter, I said, "Would you like breakfast, too?" She blinked, stood up, and five minutes later sat on the kitchen floor holding out Cheerios to Sunny and Rocky. She put one handful into her mouth. "I have to help Rocky eat his," she said. I watched with admiration and could only conclude that children have ways of dealing with loss that adults regretfully learn to disregard.

Could I get back enough innocence in small measures to create a world that felt safe to enter? I didn't know.

That afternoon, Erika held up the book *Henry Huggins* by Beverly

Cleary, selected from the family room bookshelf. She asked if we could read it together. I breathed deeply while we settled on the sofa, and I opened it to where Brian had written his name on the inside cover: twice and in cursive. He had read it many times, and the three of us had turned the last page again and again. Determined to avoid being launched into past memories I couldn't deal with, I focused on Erika's enthusiasm. Near the end of the first page, she started reading it herself, definitely ready to enjoy the story to the end.

What made the book such a classic for my son and now held delight for my daughter? Brian loved giving comfort through humor, just as Henry did through the experiences of caring for the stray dog, Ribsy. At a young age, Brian seemed to instinctively understand that paying it forward was part of a healthy self.

I wanted that same health and happiness for the three of us: *lives with confidence and purpose.*

Brian and Erika used to help with the household chores of organizing clothes and books, sweeping and dusting, and cleaning up after meals. Those memories lingered, and I didn't know how to bring the positive feelings back without Brian. Absent one word from me, Erika made her bed, folded her laundry, and picked up books and other items left on the furniture and the floor.

I cleaned the three levels of our house once a week, prepared meals, and kept my daughter on schedule for her gymnastics class and playdates. Part of me said the solitary work was a way to hang onto some normalcy. I couldn't risk letting in memories of dusting the piano and bookshelves with both children.

Oskar's pattern of asking for or accepting help to pull weeds or wash the cars appeared to trigger his pain, too. He yanked out blackberry vines, kept the garage organized, and spent hours sharpening tools, mostly by himself. If Erika stood in front of him with her little garden gloves, he would say, "Maybe you can help next time."

One day when my husband and I were alone, I started to share feelings about missing Brian, but getting minutes of blankness, I stopped. This wasn't the right time. Evenings when my daughter and I took walks through our hillside, we invited her dad to join us. He always chose to stay with a household task. I knew it was best to be sensitive, patient, and kind, watch his body language, and listen for any emotion he expressed. This kind of subtlety seemed to be working with Erika.

One afternoon, in the middle of raking cut blackberry vines, Oskar set his tools against a fir tree and called to me. In a matter-of-fact tone, he suggested a hike up a local butte. I was overjoyed by his willingness to reach out, if not for himself, for his daughter and me. Some of the time during the five-mile hike, Erika and I walked beside him and made comments like, "See all the Oregon grape plants" and "If we come in winter, there will be white berries on the snowberries." We got only a blink of acknowledgment as we reached the top of the butte. There, during this pleasant mid-August afternoon, the fresh air and view of surrounding mountains brought smiles to Erika and me, and occasional half-smiles to Oskar.

Without a gesture, he jogged his way down a different trail. Almost running to keep up, my daughter and I glanced at trees, ferns, and flowers. At the car, I recapped how energizing the hike felt. Erika asked if we could come again tomorrow. Her father only blinked, pressing his lips tight. Back home, he appeared stone-faced as he finished raking, extracting poison oak, and planting shrubs.

* *

To those who weren't our close friends, we were the "normal-as-can-be-expected family." Hypothetically, it was true, but the characterization bothered me. Although I pretended otherwise, it was becoming harder to believe in a state approaching normalcy following the death of a child. My emotions ran the gamut of *everything will eventually be okay* to *I'll never come to terms with Brian's death.* The fact that I would always miss my son was beyond consideration.

I felt Erika was dealing with her brother's loss by getting back into the water, staying close to his cat, and talking with her Playskool dolls. Oskar offered no insight regarding feelings about his son, and very little about anything else.

EIGHT
ERIKA SWIMS FORWARD

On our fourth day home, our neighbor friend Erik knocked at our front door, the visit arranged through his mom, Gayle. Erika grinned at the five-year-old with thick, dark-blond hair swinging his sand bucket. "Can you play?" My two children and Erik had spent the previous summer climbing trees, collecting bugs, and throwing pebbles into the creek below our greenbelt forest. At a picnic the week before we left for Europe, Brian had told his friend he would see him in a month.

Erika invited Erik inside, collected her own bucket, and said, "Mom, I'm going to play." While I watched from the deck, they skipped down the path toward the creek. At the height of rain and snow, it held two to three inches of water but today was dry.

Erika stopped midway and looked up at me with a questioning expression.

I waved in a do-it-if-you-are-comfortable gesture, while Erik squealed that he had found a stone with three colors.

My daughter ran to look, then crouched a few feet away and held up a pebble. "This one sparkles like glitter."

Together, the two friends giggled through several more discoveries.

Later, they set their buckets on the steps and came inside to eat crackers, feed bits to the dollhouse people, and put them to bed.

The next day, during our lunch on the deck, Erik called to Erika from the foot of the maple with two trunks. She swallowed the last of her sandwich and ran to her friend's side. I rearranged dining room hutch dishes where I could hear the pair climbing. When I could no longer pick up their cheerful voices, I went out and peered downward. The kids sat on low branches with Sunny beside them, their faces solemn, my daughter speaking softly. I didn't ask her about that conversation, but recently, Erik said that Erika had told him everything that happened at the Inn River. "I've never forgotten any of it," he said while reiterating his enjoyment of the days spent inspecting rocks and climbing trees.

The two passed July, August, and September afternoons "camping" in the woods and playing hide-and-seek while the squirrels darted between the oaks. The buckets of pretty rocks stayed next to the maple.

I took it as a stage of healing that my daughter could play, confide in a friend, and love nature again. She didn't have Brian to bury beneath the tree, but she had his cat who scampered into the high branches and came back to rest beside her.

As adults, Oskar and I could find numerous reasons to avoid play, keep deep feelings hidden, and not fully participate in nature's restorative gifts. In some respects, that accommodates staying with the grief. I asked myself how long either of us could take the constant reminder of our life as a foursome.

One Monday in early August, I washed windows while Erik and Erika raced Matchbox cars on our back deck. The kids pushed the cars off again, and then I heard the comment, "We get to go swimming today." Erika jumped up and ran to find her suit. I caught up with her and learned that Erik had heard his mother and me talking. It was clear my daughter was eager to be in the water again. I brushed hair away from her face and asked if she could wait until Friday. I needed time to deal with my drowning fears since there would be no lifeguard where Erika would swim.

Four days later, outside the gate to our private community pool, I remembered how Brian and I used to stand at the flowering hydrangeas. He would sniff and say, "They smell like candy." Today, I heard laughter and splashing from kids already swimming and willed myself to open the gate. With our children ready to run to the shallow end, Gayle and I clasped their hands and repeated our safety message. They nodded and stiffened their small bodies to walk to the steps and wade into the water.

Erika tossed a ball to Erik, and the back-and-forth continued, interspersed with dog-paddling. Then she said to him, "Watch me swim." She did the crawl stroke across the shallow end while I walked beside her. Erik took in every motion and soon stood next to his friend, extending his arm and drawing it back. Erika practiced the movement with him, and when he continued on his own, she swam back and forth across the pool. Her strokes and kicks got better every time. The two kids swam forward together for several years.

Gayle was a strong swimmer, but I kept that thought away. I was thankful I found courage on my own not to ask her to "be ready."

Erika liked the idea of celebrating her August birthday with Hilary, a Portland friend's daughter who had the same date. Caroline and I thought the adventure could be enjoyable for both girls. Soon after we settled in at the family's lakeside home, the two girls eagerly tore off gift wrappings of more dolls and toys than they could count. Lost for hours in play, they only managed a few bites of pizza and cake.

Although we had been with this family on several occasions, Oskar stood mostly by himself when the adults gathered to talk and eat. To help him feel welcome, Caroline, her husband, and other guests commented about the temperate weather and how engaged the little girls seemed to be. My husband nodded, but it was clear he would have preferred to stay at home. When Erika gave him her new Raggedy Ann doll to hold, he asked her the doll's name. She put its face toward him and said, "Raggedy Ann, of course."

Caroline and I played house with the girls, and then my friend suggested a short motorboat ride with the two girls. She said it would be good for Erika. I was petrified at first, but with my life vest fastened and my hand never leaving the float cushion under me, I relaxed a bit as we made our way along the quiet lake. Later, I stood on the beach to let water wash over my feet, grateful that Erika could again enjoy water. I had to fight away thoughts that Brian would never celebrate moments like this.

At home that night, I closed the bedroom door and knelt at a window. Erika's ability to enjoy pleasant experiences impressed me. My hands folded, I meditated on these scenes until I could express out loud how fortunate I was to have her as my daughter. She deserved 100 percent of my support and strength to grow and thrive.

NINE
BRIAN'S LEGACY

It was the second week of August, and a hint of vanilla drifted from the clematis bush toward the picnic table. I set the two plates with PBJ sandwiches and carrot sticks next to each other while Erika placed the milk glasses and sipped from hers. We paired tasty bites with listening to robins singing from the trees and watching deer nap in the canyon. Erika crunched her last carrot, opened her dollhouse, and said, "I have to feed the girl and her friend." She knelt to pick up the dolls.

Rings from the kitchen wall phone jingled to the deck, and I went to answer.

"Hello."

"Is this Mrs. Janice Jensen?"

"Yes, it is."

"My name is Mr. Hamlin. I'm with the Citizen Services Department of the American Embassy in Seattle. I am so sorry about the drowning of your son." He then relayed the stunning information that the body of a boy between eight and eleven years old had been recovered in Munich.

Outside, I heard dollhouse people thud to the deck. I knew that the Inn River flowed northeast and connected with tributaries large and small. The embassy's information offered a measure of hope that we could bring Brian home, but I shuddered at the knowledge that my son's body had been tossed about for this long a time. Could reopening the wounds that had barely begun to heal be the right choice?

I breathed several times to space out the information and thread it into words that gave me direction. Although it seemed unlikely that Brian would have gotten so far north on a river with so many forks, it was possible. My hand trembled, and I looked at Erika tending to her dolls. "May I have a number to call you back in five minutes?"

I grabbed a cloth from under the sink and went to my daughter, stroking her soft hair. I said, "I'll bet the little people would enjoy a nap in the sun while you clean their house." She gazed into the structure, her chest rising and falling. I smiled and told her I would be just inside and come to get her soon. She gave me a pensive nod.

I closed the sliding door and watched Erika sit, move the doll beds to the table, and lay the little people down on them. Then she faced the plastic house and rubbed the cloth across its roof.

It was painful to linger over my son's final moments or the condition of his body after almost two months. I went back to the kitchen, stretched my arms upward, then bent to touch my toes. Willing myself to listen and ask questions, I dialed the number. "Hamlin speaking."

"Mrs. Jensen, again, and thank you for your call. Was this child found quite recently?"

He told me he was notified a day ago by the embassy in Munich via the Vienna office.

The door opened quietly, and I saw Erika, with furrowed brow, tiptoe to the cupboard for the spray bottle. I waited for her to close the door. Technology associated with identifying remains was basic in 1972, but I asked, "Do you have details about the ethnicity, nationality, or condition of the child?"

I was then told the embassy had only been given the age range and gender identity of male.

I paused and sat down. It could be Brian.

"Mrs. Jensen, are you still there?"

"Yes."

"I am sure this news is disturbing. But if you will tell me whether or not to proceed with identification, I will notify the Munich office."

Erika pressed her nose against the glass. Should we go to Munich and make certain the authorities have the correct data? I informed Mr. Hamlin I would call him after I spoke with my husband. I said goodbye and went to admire the dolls who were still resting on the picnic table. "After their nap, I washed their beds, their faces, and the bottoms of their feet," my daughter said, eyeing me with curiosity.

I sat down on the bench, picked up the girl doll's friend, and held him. Erika wrapped her hands around the daughter, the mother, and the father. She told me the dolls were hungry again, so we fed them, playing house until it was time to fix dinner.

I couldn't help but draw a contrast between the dollhouse family and ours. In the pretend world, the routines and feelings could be configured and dealt with according to a desired storyline. Erika and I could playact our way through scene after scene and assign emotions that moved us through the story. Painful reactions could be handled in a few words or replaced.

I prayed that playacting could transfer a measure of resolution into our real world. Maybe scenes close to reality would let us find comfort and a path forward.

Concerned about how my husband would be affected by the news, I hesitated to tell him about the discovery. He had only referred to the tragedy when it was necessary and with the fewest words possible. But I needed his input. I spoke with my neighbor and friend Gayle, who agreed that it would not be healing or helpful for either Oskar or me to go to Munich. Further dialogue with the embassy confirmed that dental records were the most reliable method of identification. I needed to find an appropriate time to talk with Oskar. I waited and waited for the moment.

To take my mind off the Munich discovery, I filled the mid-August days with completing summer projects, including the removal of furniture for carpet cleaning. I rehung the framed baby photos of Brian and Erika on the wall above the armchairs and, with folded hands, offered them as a practical test toward forward-looking memories. In contrast, to mitigate the pain of never-again breakfasts and lunches with our foursome, I removed a chair from the kitchen nook. At first, I felt like a traitor, but I finally understood my motive as helping us process.

We had not seriously considered counseling as a couple—or taking Erika. In the 1970s, grief and children's counseling was hardly even a concept, never mind a program. Our pastor friend, Dan, had been a steady sounding board for questions and expressions, which mostly came from me, and I had consulted other trusted professionals. I felt this to be the best level of life and normalcy right now.

The third week of August and five weeks after returning from Austria, Oskar was reading the newspaper from his blue chair while I started *Watership Down*. It seemed the right time to talk about the Munich information. I asked how work was going, and said our daughter looked forward to starting school. Then, I led into a summary of my embassy interactions, reiterating Erika's request to bury her brother by the maple tree. Oskar folded his newspaper, set it on his lap, and faced me without blinking. Then he simply nodded, his lips pursed and cheeks taut.

"So, you agree that we should proceed with the identification for Erika's sake, and probably ours, too?"

"Yes."

We both felt the dental records should be hand delivered and tried to think of people going to the upcoming Munich Olympic Games. The next few days, Oskar carried on with his tasks without any outward signs of extra stress over the discovery. I spent mine contacting friends who might be going to Europe, forgetting where I had left a dust cloth or my keys. The details of the drowning and the possible scenarios regarding how the body would have gotten to Munich kept me awake for nights. I paced the living room, peered out windows into the dark night, and many evenings, wrapped myself in a blanket to sit on the deck. Finally, when dawn came and I had done several yoga poses, I could consider possible responses.

Five days after telling Oskar, and just before he drifted off into sleep, he said, "Joe from my office is going to Munich for the Olympic Games. Maybe he could take the records." Three days later, Joe and his wife left carrying the X-rays. Would bringing Brian home, if indeed it was him, help my husband heal? I wasn't sure.

In the third week of September, Mr. Hamlin called. "Mrs. Jensen, the dental records were not a match."

I regretted that my little girl would never be comforted by her brother's physical presence, but I was relieved at not having to face the sadness of a cemetery burial. On a stroll near our dry creek, I picked up a gold maple leaf splashed with red that had departed from its source. Droplets of water made it sparkle in the filtered sunlight, my fingers smoothing across the blade. The intricate vein patterns intrigued me, and I reflected on how the leaf would soon begin a new life, enriching the soil.

I bowed my head, released it, and watched it drift to the ground, acknowledging Brian's similar contribution to his river grave.

The fall months of September and October meant absorbing the new challenges into the regular schedules and commitments.

In early September, I walked my daughter up a long sidewalk to her first-grade classroom at our neighborhood school. Having home-schooled her with basic skills, as well as expanding her imagination and curiosity, I believed Erika to be well prepared. She had regularly placed her writing, number papers, and artwork on her father's desk, always looking forward to his thumbs-up.

Today, I pressed her hands between mine. She wiggled free, walked ahead, and entered her classroom while I waved to the teacher. Watching from a wall, I saw Mrs. H pass out paper for students to draw their families. Erika drew Oskar, me, and herself with our hands stretched toward each other. I moved closer when she pointed to the bottom right corner and said she would show Brian picking daisies. I kissed her and ran to my car, pressing my head to the steering wheel while tears soaked my blouse and pants.

In late September, Oskar smiled at Erika and me. In a voice that sounded heartfelt, he said, "I want to use Brian's life insurance policy as seed money for a student music scholarship." Apparently, he had given the idea deep thought and had conferenced with our insurance agent. I welcomed his desire to honor Brian in this tangible way.

After sending an invitation to friends and family to contribute, we selected a committee that included Oskar to interview the applying elementary and high school students. At the final selection meeting, my husband talked about how pleased Brian would be to honor children who shared his love of the piano and other instruments. For several weeks, his step had a vitality I hadn't seen for many months. He also created an endowment fund at his college alma mater for a mathematics scholarship that continues today.

Helping young people whom he saw as exemplifying his son's interests and talents seemed to connect Oskar to Brian. I prayed that the connections would give him some insight into the good father he truly was. How much the efforts would bring him relief from his grief and guilt, I didn't know.

At about the same time, we invited neighbors for an informal memorial in our living room. Many had wanted to grieve with us in person but instead gave us privacy and sent cards, food, and flowers. Oskar agreed to the sharing, but I was concerned that if there was much hugging, he would become uncomfortable and leave.

As I ground coffee, set out fruits, nuts, and cookies, and arranged plates and napkins, I regretted not building in time in advance to relax and reflect. A range of emotions began to fill me before everyone arrived at one o'clock, and I wondered if this lack of quiet time was a mistake.

Our kind and understanding neighbors brought us through the afternoon feeling supported and uplifted, and my husband seemed to take the afternoon in stride.

On a mid-October morning, Brian's school held an assembly to honor his memory. The faculty and students, along with our relatives and friends, filled the auditorium. The service was difficult, but the inherent energy, the tributes, and the presence of the children lent comfort and perspective. One teacher said, "Your son's quiet and unselfish love for fellow students and teachers will never leave me." A classmate spoke of Brian holding back answers to give others a turn.

After a piano recital the following spring, I wrote a letter to my son describing his musician friend Jeff's beautiful rendition of "Tarantella." I said, "You would have been pleased with every perfectly shaded tone." The letter bookmarks the piece in a piano book.

On nights when I couldn't sleep, my mind saw what would have been Brian's fourth-grade class.

Without him.

He had idolized the teacher, Mrs. Clark, and I felt him tell her it was okay that he wasn't there.

During the years Brian would have attended middle school, high school, and college, I occasionally met his friends. When Clay, a grade school friend, was a college sophomore, I saw his parents at the library, and we talked about how the two boys loved science and, in particular, living organisms. I believe Clay, now a healthcare practitioner, and Brian, a presumed engineer, would have been enduring friends.

These days, I visit with my son's classmates, who represent professions as diverse as environmental law, music, and plumbing. One of his friends said recently, "Your son gave me encouragement all those years ago that continues to make a difference."

TEN
BRIAN'S ROOM

On a Saturday morning in October, I heard a door rattle on our upper level. It was Sunny, again wanting to check if his master had come back. Not ready to open Brian's door, I had been ignoring the rattles for weeks.

That same evening, he pushed harder at the wood, and I decided to let him see for himself that his best friend hadn't come home. I faced the entrance, reached for the cold brass knob, and paused. The hesitation was familiar—I had felt it in Austria at the auto repair shop, at the swim center, and at our local community pool.

When I pressed my face against the door, I could almost hear my son playing "The Lion Sleeps Tonight" on his Dolmetsch treble recorder. The thought warmed my fingers, and I turned the knob. Standing in pajamas, Brian would face our backwoods, finger the holes, and blink on each downbeat, chuckling through what he considered "mistakes." Then, snuggling under the covers, he would wait for me to join him. His arm cradling my neck and tickling my chin, we would read together.

The second I opened the door, Sunny thrust his body forward as the smell of the reconditioned leather baseball mitt wafted to me. I used to covet the leather's scent and the scenes of catches and games it generated, but today it brought memories I couldn't handle.

Happy feelings shifted to sad. Enough bare sentiment for today. I ran down the stairs. After a few minutes, the cat appeared at his food dish, and I hoped he had found comfort in the sniffs and accepted his master's absence. I was thankful someone had closed the door by the time I came to bed.

My son was in a faraway river, but I looked forward to one day appreciating every meaningful detail of this room and his life.

Sunny pawed again and again, seemingly for reminder sniffs. After a few weeks, I let him swish against my leg and opened the door. He hurried toward the dresser top where a photo of the four of us sat between fir cones. Brian had placed it there the morning before we left for Europe. I grabbed the cat mid-leap, holding him tight. He wriggled himself to the floor, rubbed his nose against his master's slippers, and scampered to the hallway.

He seemed to sense that I was still not ready to go deeper into Brian's world.

I told Erika and Oskar about the rendezvous, not dwelling on my struggle to immerse myself in Brian's belongings and treasures. Instead, I offered how Sunny seemed to find peace in quick sniffs of slippers and a ball mitt. I asked if either of them wanted to talk about the room, and they both shook their heads. I said the cat would be happy to lead the way if the door was opened for him, and that watching him find energy in smells might be reassuring. I got no reaction from either of them.

One morning at the beginning of April, as sunshine beamed into the kitchen and dining room windows, it felt right to be part of Brian's room. I opened the door without hesitation. Drawn to the dresser, my eyes looked between the fir cones at the photo. I had to feel the depth beneath what the facial expressions told me to find the kinship and love I knew existed. Knowing my son, I can only surmise this was his way of keeping us together in spirit forever, his influence representing a collective goodness. I arranged the fir cones into a large capital B at the front of the photograph.

At the twin bed, I paused beside the quilt with tiny cornflowers hand-embroidered by my mother-in-law. Brian and I had admired each perfectly stitched shape many times. Glancing at the recorder on the nightstand brought a reminder of how many songs my son had taught me to play. "Home on the Range" was a favorite because we made up humorous new verses. I would find a way to create words and laugh again.

In a few moments, a hole on the recorder became a gigantic black cavern and my heart fell into it, unable to claw its way out. I closed my eyes, grabbed the instrument, and stuffed it under the cornflower quilt.

Grief can be like that. One instant, a recollection gives pleasure; the next it creates a void so deep it is hard to imagine climbing upward. Life is an act of constantly rebooting the journey and including the Higher Power's input, no matter the circumstances. Maybe not on an expected timeline—but at relevant moments. I had to trust each space and juncture to lead me to the next.

During late spring, I entered the room for several brief visits. On the last morning of June, I stepped to the front of the bookshelf and knelt, easing my hand across spines of the frayed titles. Jutting forward was *Banner in the Sky* by James Ramsey Ullman, the story of Rudi Matt's ascent of the Matterhorn. I slid the book out, gazed at the cover, and opened it to a sock inserted close to the end. The night before we left for Europe, my son had interrupted our evening good-night kisses with, "Please, Mom, let me skim the last pages." He and I had discussed the plot many times because we would soon hike in the Alps ourselves. I knew he wanted to find out if Rudi made it to the top. After a few minutes of fast reading, Brian called out, "Mom, he reached the summit!"

The day we arrived in Austria, we hiked foothills where blue-gray and white peaks towered. When we reached our car again, our nine-year-old turned toward the mountains. "Someday, I will climb the Matterhorn like Rudi."

I touched the cones that formed the letter "B" on the dresser and remembered Brian had called troll dolls from a Nordic store in Germany "forest creatures." He had studied their tightly wound dried grass torsos, arms, and legs; long noses, moss hair, and fingers and toes of cone pieces. I bought the pair, and for three days, my son held them up as art to his sister. He later promised to make me a forest creature of my own with his fir cones.

I formed the cones into a creature, knowing my son would honor its lopsided head, drooping eye, and uneven stick arms. It lived on my office desk until I couldn't glue the pieces back together one more time, speaking to me of beauty's diversity and individuality appearing at impactful moments.

I opened Brian's T-shirt drawer and reverently touched the bare space that had contained his blue-striped shirt, the one Erika wore hours after her brother was washed away. It occupied the center of her top drawer, and when I settled her clean shirts, I smoothed my fingers across the soft knitted cotton. This always gave me strength. Both of my children are part of this piece of cloth and part of each other.

I thought of a packing conundrum we had faced when we were getting ready for our trip, and the memory gave Brian's closet senti-mental value. We had planned to attend a Mozart concert in Salzburg honoring his favorite composer. A dress jacket was his wardrobe choice, but I finally convinced him that a sweater would be fine. If he were here today, he would say, "Don't stress about this, Mom." Pride blended with my pain.

While we folded clothes that evening, I asked Erika to let me know if she wanted to visit her brother's room with me. We did go together a few times that summer, and I occasionally found her fingering his recorder or paging through one of his books. Her look told me not to ask questions. In the fall, I picked up *Mr. Popper's Penguins* from Brian's bottom bookshelf and sat on the bed to read. Erika walked by, chose a book from the top shelf, and went downstairs to curl up on the sofa.

Spending time in Brian's room brought me to consider counseling for Erika again. Her teachers and others didn't see issues needing attention, but if there was help for submerged issues we were missing, I wanted to address them. Oskar was unsure of the value. I interviewed three professionals and once again found childhood grief therapy of the 1970s lacking. I decided to watch Erika closely for signs of distress and draw her feelings out when it seemed appropriate. My mission for her: open-mindedness and normal growth with an individual timeframe of healing.

I only found Oskar in his son's room one evening, standing in the middle, rocking forward on his toes and smoothing his hair back. He saw me and, with a sober face, turned and hurried out. I couldn't help reflecting on Brian's plea, "Save Erika." I hoped Oskar would come to understand on every level that he had tried his hardest to save both his children.

During a pleasant July afternoon, the second full summer home, I studied Brian's drawings of big ships, rivers, sailboats, and Old Faithful. I touched the maple "helicopters" taped to the walls. That evening, Erika brightened when she talked about drawing airplanes and cars with Brian using his colored pencils. She also said, "Dad, remember how you and Brian read about what makes the maple seed helicopters fly?" Oskar smiled his straight-lipped smile and smoothed his hair.

I visited Brian's room regularly over the next three years. Every item stayed where he had placed it, and I dusted around the photo and the maple seeds. The moments increased when I could let my mind wander freely and identify happy memories of my son's treasures, belongings, and life. When a memory turned sad, sometimes I left before it overtook the joy. But other times, I let myself feel the pain. I didn't want to discard a detail of anything that was meaningful.

On a spring day, I discovered his handmade felt angel ornament tucked into a book as a place marker. He had hung it on our holiday tree the Christmas before the trip to Europe. Oskar had started singing "Hark! The Herald Angels Sing," and Erika placed her bell-shaped ornament near Brian's angel—the one that contained the photo of her grinning through two missing teeth.

The memory brought me to the holiday piano duets Brian and I played where Sunny switched his tail over the music from the top of the console. The first time I thought about it, I vowed to chuckle— and keep chuckling. And I have.

Each day gave me insight. And when I now look back to the beginning of my life and how I followed my instincts to marry Oskar and have children, to the aftermath of the tragedy and this moment, Brian's love and compassion keep reappearing. Small everyday joys have burst through my subconscious to bring relief from grief.

One day during the fifth summer, before I packed up Brian's room for a move to a fresh start, I picked up the photograph from his dresser and again studied our faces. The image of being together forever in spirit and love gave me goosebumps of hope.

Yes! That was the right image. I held the photo to my chest, knelt, and challenged myself to believe every day, *there will always be four*. I knew that somehow, we each would persistently find each other, just as we did on trails in the rhododendron park the day the picture was taken.

ELEVEN
STRIVING FOR NORMALCY

During our first full summer home, Erika's upbeat nature and funny stories about Brian and his cat helped cheer us up. She remembered that when Sunny was bored, he unrolled toilet paper until Brian collected a jar with fresh ants, releasing them one at a time for him to paw. The ant chase went on until the last one had disappeared. Oskar shook his head at the humor. I prepared my son's favorite dish of brown rice with cheese and tomatoes every few weeks. Erika and I scooped healthy helpings and smacked our lips.

My daughter made new friends in our neighborhood, invited girls from her class to ride bikes, and presented pictures of favorite leotard styles and colors to her gymnastics classmates. She enjoyed her piano teacher, a lively sixtyish woman, and practiced daily. We occasionally played duets, which took me back to my mother and learning the two parts of "Barcarolle" from *Tales of Hoffman*. Erika and I eventually mastered the music, the piece becoming a favorite of three generations.

〜

I received my master's degree in curriculum and instruction in June of 1973 and celebrated with a party and a champagne toast to making dreams come true. Two weeks later, the three of us went to Disneyland. Erika and Oskar wanted to enjoy the Matterhorn Bobsleds in honor of Brian's interest in the mountain, and Erika and I chose the Pirates of the Caribbean to honor Halloween. Cream-cheese-filled pretzels were an evening treat.

The first two days, Oskar engaged with the rides and events, but by the third, he had become quiet and let Erika and me choose the adventures. The next morning, he wanted to leave at noon. We did. It was hard to ignore his darkening mood, and I suggested a walk at a nearby park. He told us he was ready to drive home.

In the middle of August that same summer, twenty-five family members and friends gathered for a reunion campout at mile-high Waldo Lake in the Oregon Cascades. The group had suggested postponing the trip until the next summer, but Erika was eager to play hide-and-seek in the woods with her cousins, skip rocks at the shore, and splash her uncles from a canoe. Oskar quietly approved the trip, picnics, and water fun with family and close friends. His two brothers invited him to repeat the hike around the lake.

First and foremost, I kept my angst at bay about facing uncomfortable memories of Waldo Lake itself. Its deepness had always concerned me when Oskar or another adult paddled a canoe with Brian or Erika to Rhododendron Island, a healthy distance away and out of binocular range. I knew this time Erika and her father would paddle their new raft around corners I couldn't monitor.

We arrived midafternoon at Islet Campground, and after camp setup, I went to the water. I had to come to terms with it and allow my daughter to wade beyond the shore rocks into the lake and paddle a raft or canoe. Images of previous trips swept over me: Brian and Erika standing knee-deep as blue-gray ripples washed against their legs while they giggled and shivered.

I walked over smooth rocks and around the scattered sharp ones to watch a light breeze send small waves across the pristine lake.

When I stepped on pebbles and sand, thoughts carried me back to the Inn. I shoved the memory away and focused on being here for Erika and Oskar, determined to make the most of the four days. A woodpecker tapped on Doug fir bark nearby, and a mountain chickadee chirped and trilled from a branch. I breathed deeply and sat down on a log. One part of me said, *Stay at the beach and enjoy the solitude and memories.* But the happy thoughts began to mix with what was missing. I turned and stumbled through the woods, taking a long route back to the camp.

While I walked, a new thought struck me: *Oskar is a good swimmer, and he did save his daughter. He will take care of her.* I relaxed for now.

The next morning, my husband and daughter inflated the Sevylor raft they had purchased a week earlier. Erika was set on paddling the length of the long lake, or at least most of it, but knew I could only handle a short ride. In the hot sun, I forced myself to sit on the rubber floor in the back and grip the oarlocks. With every small wave, I clung more tightly, and at the first sight of liverwort swaying or trout darting, my knuckles went white. Soon, sweat poured down me. Oskar saw I was merely enduring the trip, and after he had rowed up the lake for ten minutes, he turned and headed back. The second the raft touched pebbles, I jumped out and bowed with my hands folded.

I didn't know if I could ever do it again. Maybe when I learned to dance on water.

Erika said to her dad, "Tomorrow, can we row all the way to Rhododendron Island?" They did, and I saw the first half of their paddle strokes through the binoculars. It was obvious they took in every ripple, wave, and zigzagging fish with pleasure. When the Sevylor was back on shore, my daughter hopped out and ran to me.

"I pretended you were with us, Mom." That comment was precious, and her love swelled my gratitude that her father had made it happen.

The experience seemed to have created a fresh bond between Erika and Oskar. I wanted to believe he let himself feel enjoyment.

Sometimes during the four days, he walked less stiffly and relaxed his arms, but often his lips puckered. When his brother asked if he was having some moments of fun, Oskar looked at his feet, mouthing a quiet, "One or two."

During July the next summer, my husband decided to replace the moss-green outside house paint with sienna-rust and restain the back deck. This honored his hardwired heritage of cleanliness, organization, and dedication to a home's prime condition.

We pressure-washed the three stories, spray-painted two coats, and brushstroked the trim. When we had finished, he stood on the front lawn and said, "One more job off my list." I enjoyed watching him throw himself into this project and showed my gratitude by making cheese soufflé. Erika called it yummy while her dad gave the traditional Norwegian thank-you, *"Takk for maten."*

When his mother, two brothers, and their families visited in September, a favorite entrée of vegetable lasagna and baby spinach tossed with candied ginger dressing got everyone cheering the joys of family celebrations. We had often gathered for birthdays, Norwegian and American holidays, and just to be together.

Every time Bestemor's specialty, Norwegian soft cake, was served with its layers of strawberries and cream and almond paste covering, oohs and aahs filled the room. Since Austria, Oskar had usually only nodded and blinked at food he liked, even the favorite soft cake.

On one occasion, his lips closed straight across his face when his younger brother said, "Our love for each other is rich like this cake." I looked into the eyes of each extended family member and once more felt their devotion and loyalty. Later, both brothers told my husband about the caring thoughts they sent to him every day. After they finished, he walked away without even a look of *I care about you, too.* I prayed Oskar would believe the sentiments so honestly expressed. Such occasions could not change what had happened, but every moment of connection could be a step toward turning an unwanted memory into something more.

The next Sunday, the two of us went for a walk in our forest, and I commented that we were blessed to have friends and family who supported our healing in every possible way. I named each person as our benefactor. Oskar nodded in agreement but didn't add to what I said.

My husband didn't appear willing or able to talk about the tragedy, making it hard to understand if and how he was processing his grief. Reflecting back through the days since we met, I realized that nothing he had ever said or done caused me to believe that pressing him to open up would have helped. Early in our relationship, when I queried him for feedback about subjects from A to Z, he usually stated facts that could be proven. If he let a hint of emotion creep in, it was to emphasize a perceived truth. His shoulders squared, his face serious, and his voice businesslike, he might say, "Your new red coat is longer and looks slimmer than the old one," or, "Research confirms the facts about . . ."

Regarding Brian or Erika's skills and accomplishments, he usually smiled mostly with his eyes and tried to animate his voice. The compliments related to how a ball was caught, whether a drawing depicted a real robin, or how long a breath was held under water. Without expecting notice or comment, he kept our kitchen drawers sliding smoothly, light bulbs replaced, and gifts of clothes, books, and money coming. For him, these were the avenues to showing love.

The music scholarship recipients were based on verified skill and verified need, which spoke to Oskar's love of his son's talents, skills, and concern for others. Firstborn and carrying the Jensen name, Brian had become Oskar's legacy. Oskar's own place in the cosmos had been somewhat restored by the scholarship.

I was left to interpret the specifics of what he meant the night he asked me to marry him. "I'm in love" were the only words spoken. I have never regretted saying, *yes*, having come to terms with who he was and would always be.

Although he and I had differing views on many subjects, we appreciated each other's intellect. He was a traditional Norwegian man—solid, independent, and trustworthy, his do-it-yourself ethos firm. I was an American with a more liberal point of view, no less trustworthy but more trusting.

Before the accident, when the kids were tucked into bed, Oskar often got comfortable in his blue chair and read history and war books. *The Longest Day* by Cornelius Ryan was one of his favorites. I sat with a cup of tea and worked my way through titles like Homer's *Odyssey*. Evening quiet time also found us fielding parenting goals that spanned conservative to more progressive, the pros and cons of government funding of certain programs, and what free will meant to a lifestyle.

Oskar's political views would remain conservative while mine would stay progressive, but we acknowledged that both of our ideologies had strengths. We agreed about paradigms for our children's education as well as details of how honesty and integrity should play out and added elements of spirituality we found relevant. Our in-sync policymaking and business structure included buying a house and caring for it; establishing reserves to give our children opportunities for art, music, and science; and saving for college and our future.

I was in charge of the household care, daily schedules, and food preparation. Oskar wrote the monthly checks, but we made joint decisions about medium to large purchases, landscape updates, and house repairs. Yard care was a family effort.

My husband had a strong interest in defining broad financial goals for our family and thoroughly researched the possibilities. This came to include both our incomes and clear-thinking investments. I was an equal partner in the final decisions.

The most important element in our relationship was respect for each other and for our differences. If the issue wasn't crucial and a decision needed to be made, we agreed to disagree, and one of us stepped up. If it was crucial, we considered a compromise. If that didn't happen, one of us made the decision. I didn't need to subscribe to the political party or to the job-related dynamics Oskar held. Instead, I focused on the solid, honorable commitment he had to his beliefs. And with most areas of our lives, we had "ballpark agreements."

∽

When conversation became increasingly difficult after Austria, I turned to books about healing from grief, took walks, and regularly questioned God. I slowly opened up to friends and clergy and later found a therapist who helped me gain a measure of insight. These avenues kept my emotions somewhat balanced, but no day or night went by when I didn't ponder what I could do, or could have done earlier, to help my marriage partner be more accessible. The intent of his messages since the accident often confused me, and sometimes

I was hard-pressed not to see them as a personal attack or a deeply buried blame game.

Oskar remained in charge of the tasks he saw as his job. I could count on him to cut the nandina bushes and trim Erika's bangs. But when her friend didn't invite her to a party, and when she cried after a piano recital performance, her father simply bowed his head. Before the tragedy, he might have attempted a word of reassurance. Through my own tears, I prayed for his understanding and tried to give her extra comfort.

If my husband had carried forward his attempts to be upbeat with Erika and me somewhat routinely as he did at Disneyland, Waldo Lake, and with friends, I would have believed he had begun to function as the partner I remembered. Our early goal was to keep processing the grief, pursue healing emotions, and eventually cast the sorrow as one element of life. Although Oskar's brothers and mother didn't make it an open issue, they hoped and prayed he would start to share his feelings about the accident, about being Brian's father, and how he was coping with that role.

Losing a child means life will be forever different. I knew that. And the grieving process is as individual as the timeframe, but our choices do move the journey forward, maintain the status quo, or take us backward.

I hoped sharing thoughts about life and its incentivizing forces, gathering with family and friends, walking, or painting a house would help us find strength to go forward. When I suggested that counseling could let us openly express our heartbreak, my husband's face turned almost white and he uttered a firm, "No." Grief counseling, even for adults, was in its infancy at the time, so I didn't pursue it.

I was left to figure out if and how Oskar was processing his son's death. The times I tried to encourage even one comment, he could not give a hint about his feelings. He was also silent about his role in Erika's and my journey.

The more I researched the scientific premise and natural rhythms of people's efforts to live in harmony, the more I understood how choices I made drove my own destiny and that of others—or stopped them. To be sure, our present family relationships didn't parallel the spirited ones they once were, but for the three of us to survive and blossom, I had to seize every opportunity, small and large. My goal was for Oskar, Erika, and me to find our thriving selves once again.

I revisited the happier times often: the early years of our marriage in Seattle and the first three-and-a-half in Oregon with a partner who worked hard, two children who loved nature, and a blessed energy surrounding the four of us.

TWELVE
GIVING AND RECEIVING

Although my roles as mother and wife were central to my life, I needed productive energy to fill me during the school day, so with my master's degree in hand and Erika in second grade, I returned to teaching in September 1973. I was thrilled to be the teacher for twenty-seven first graders with my daughter in the classroom next door.

On a cold morning in January, my student Jack shivered outside the front door when I arrived. He showed me his brother's book *The Monkey and the Bee*, by Leland Jacobs, an early reader written in rhyme with a few "big words." Jack said, "I can read it," but his face told me that he didn't believe his own story. I sat with him during spare moments until he could sight-read or sound out every word. He took the book home again and read it to his brother. The following morning, he was waiting for me, grinning from under a wool hat that almost covered his eyes. "I'm as smart as my brother," he said. I was proud, too, then and every other time I helped a student break the reading code.

In the spring, my students and I planted bean seeds in Styrofoam cups. We poked four holes in the bottom, scooped in soil, and buried two seeds near the center. The kids poured small amounts of water over the soil. With dirt clinging to her hand, Sybil rubbed her eyes and said, "My doggie got buried, too." I sat down and put my arm around her. She told me how her cocker spaniel, Red, was run over, and her dad made a grave in their backyard. I told her I understood how much she missed Red, but that he was nearby, and she could talk to him when she needed to feel him with her.

A friend visited with her new Lhasa terrier about the same time, and we fell in love with the dog, who happened to have a brother looking for a forever family. Erika begged for her own puppy. Oskar and I agreed the dog would add another dimension of friendship to Erika's life. She named him Pempa after the Tibetan canine in one of Brian's favorite books, *Daughter of the Mountains*. Erika, Erik, and neighbor Robin invented tricks to teach him. When my class had Pets Day, Sybil introduced her new shelty, Brownie, who rolled over twice. Erika visited with Pempa and signaled him to stand on his hind feet. Both doggies got a treat, and Erika and I savored the bond that reaching out created.

In the late fall of 1973, friends invited Oskar and me to help at a soup kitchen. At first, we both excused ourselves, saying we couldn't make the time. But the requests continued to come through church bulletins and on community boards, and I couldn't dismiss the desperate need. *Could I add the pain and suffering of these homeless people to my ongoing grief?* I decided to try it for one hour, one time. I would peel vegetables for a soup and cook rice and beans for a casserole; then I would leave.

I drove around and around the site asking myself, *Is this right for me?* Finally, I ran through pouring rain into the kitchen, completed my assigned tasks, and put on my coat. I hastily walked past the seventy men and women lined up at the door. When I pulled my car back, someone waved at me to stop. One of the key servers hadn't shown up.

I found myself dishing soup to folks wearing two or three

summer jackets and sports shoes that squished from being soaked. I held each full bowl in my outstretched hand and, without thinking, said, "Enjoy every spoonful." On the drive home, I thought about these folks and their difficult lives. My stomach ached, and I had nightmares for days picturing the camps they lived in and the bridges they curled up under, crying out for food and warmth.

The images took me to Brian and his possible pleas for help. Although pleas for help can be put into categories, each cry is personal and bears an individual's needs. Pain is pain, and loss is loss.

I remembered my son's compassion. I would add these soup kitchen folks to my prayers. During the middle of winter, I couldn't ignore the urge to go back to the kitchen. When the crowd lined up at the door, I steeled myself. I didn't know which pain was worse, feeling the suffering of these people or my own sorrow.

The desire to help grew, and although I was busy, I went back every time I had a spare hour. One evening, a very thin older man clutched a folded blanket and said, "Every person who receives this gift should hug the giver and connect hearts." Bad dreams or not, I felt compassion and comfort.

When I told Oskar the man's story, he said, "He sounds nice."

Season after season for several years, Erika and I planned and took walks and hikes, a conscious choice for spiritual guidance. Oskar joined us about half the time. We spent lovely Saturdays climbing diverse peaks, watching cougars or bobcats, identifying trees, and listening to red-breasted nuthatches. God's message came through: He created all of it with love and enjoyment of each other. I wrote a letter to God thanking him and read it out loud on one hike. Erika smiled, and Oskar patted his daughter's knee.

Teaching, working at the soup kitchen, and being part of my church group that organized classes and activities for adults and children kept me involved with people. These involvements mitigated my concerns about the role others could play in healing. But I knew that stepping back into my diverse professional and social routines would be a gradual process. There were too many unknowns about how I would react to the myriad looks and inquiries. This was the 1970s when news traveled more or less at the discretion of its source. Today, it would be impossible to keep Brian's accident known only to a few people.

At school district meetings, afraid of running into teaching colleagues I hadn't seen since the accident, I arrived after meetings started and sat at a distance. I left before anyone could speak to me. I was sure some folks' sympathy would translate to a look of horror, and others would ask, "How are your kids?" I had stayed away from social functions, such as the benefit reception for the art center where Brian had taken classes, believing I wasn't ready for questions about my artistic son.

More time would allow me to figure out how to respond in each circumstance. The Higher Power was close by, but He wanted me to turn the corners where and when it felt right.

THIRTEEN
FRIENDS

Beginning the first week back from Europe, Gayle and other women friends had taken my hand and said, "I'm here to listen and whatever else helps." In a sense, the unruffled side of me was easier to show, especially when I talked about the less stressful, practical details of family life and how I had made them meaningful to three people.

With more distant friends, my mother's philosophy, *be stoic until you shouldn't*, saw me talking about how fast the trees were growing and how much gas cost. My confidants understood that at the end of a long day, I was too tired to talk, and sometimes, in the middle of one, I was upset. On the days I carried grieving front and center, I kept the complaints to myself.

When was the right time to bring up feelings about missing Brian, how could I relate to Oskar and Erika, and when should I push toward future goals? I didn't know. And I was sure my thoughts and feelings would change as more deeply buried ones began to surface. Although I wasn't casting my personal healing as top priority, I couldn't let it slip into oblivion. I sensed that if, over the weeks, months, and years, I didn't at least maintain a level of emotional health, my recovery would be more complex and severely impact my relationships with Erika and Oskar.

Withholding my feelings gnawed at me. I finally decided to open up to my women friends and ask questions when thoughts surfaced. The soup kitchen experience showed me I could handle limited kinds of reaching out and sharing. These women continued to follow my lead in setting the amount and degree of depth we explored, but during the second late winter, I started to ask how they saw my everyday life playing out and what steps I should take to enhance my relationship with Erika and Oskar.

During a spring 1974 ski trip with our neighbor friends, Doug, Gayle, and Erik, I let deep thoughts surface to Gayle. We had angled down a steep slope, traversing several moguls, and I displayed some degree of finesse. Halfway to the bottom, I hit a large mogul and tumbled over its top. Snow and ice stuck to my lashes and cap. I blinked my eyes clear and stared at my skis. My tall friend helped me up, and we walked the rest of the way. At the lodge, we forked chicken salads, and I said, "Can I share some other big bumps I'm facing?"

I was hesitant to ask her about my relationship with Brian, but I did. Although I had enjoyed short, happy remembrances, I told her I worried I would never be fully joyful again about my son or life in general. If I continued to struggle with the memories of him, I couldn't heal enough to honor the stellar person he had been or be deeply invested in the lives of my husband, daughter, other family members, and friends.

Gayle reminded me that I often used to name the qualities I admired in Oskar and my children—the small things. She said, "Maybe if you revisited these qualities and added different characteristics over time, you could freshly embrace the sentiments." She also suggested I write diary pages of active grieving for both painful and pleasant situations. I hugged her for her perceptive input and told her I would continue to seek the right counselor.

Talking to Gayle helped me reach out to a teaching colleague, a person with a great capacity to listen. Vi asked pointed questions such as, "Are you taking time away from your busy life to relax and reflect?" I told her I occasionally did, but it was obvious that those times were so rare that they weren't contributing to my well-being.

One day I felt particularly stilted and stuck. I told Vi I wanted a fresh vision of where I was going and why, but I couldn't articulate the details. She listened intently and helped me plan a solo visit to my mother, brother, and friends in Seattle. With Mom, I strolled the multicolored iris garden she had continued to plant and listened to her counsel. She advised me to release the experiences and feelings that felt right. Her hand in mine, she said, "Keep seeking those hard answers." I value that trip to this day.

On a Sunday morning in May, my neighbor Marlene invited me to walk through her beautiful garden with its blooming shrubs. Near the pink hydrangeas, she asked if Oskar was able to express *any* feelings about the accident. She wasn't surprised when I recounted how he still shut down every time I said a word about our son.

As I stood in front of a Sundance Mexican orange display, lovely with its yellow leaves and white flowers, my mind reflected on the spirit of Mexico's Day of the Dead festival. *If only the symbolism of celebrating the dead with a festival could, in a small way, grant Oskar a celebration of Brian.*

My friend said, "No one can grieve for another." This statement helped me let go of some of the tension I felt about my husband's silence.

I fingered the Rose Glow Japanese barberry bush, with its burgundy leaves splashed with pink and cream. My lovely German neighbor said, "These blossoms and shrubs are always here for your reflection—just come. And I'll be inside." I made solo visits over the next months and years. Each time I brushed my fingers over the solid, leathery barberry leaves, I felt a stronger sense of belonging to nature and received healing gifts.

Reaching out to my women friends—and to Gayle's husband, Doug, and our friend, Pastor Dan—enabled me to see that this group took life in stride, no matter what the circumstance or difficulty. I was fortunate to call these well-balanced, articulate people my friends.

My German and English ethnic heritage brought decisiveness and endurance from my parents, who taught me to carry through with what I believed and knew to be right. Professional training in child development and parenting gave me confidence to pursue decisions that benefited Erika and extended to Oskar and myself.

Some insights were only possible through intuition and faith. That meant I had to take risks without knowing the outcome. Prayer, meditation, and inspirational reading became an integral part of each day. I would work to learn from every source and carry on through the mistakes.

FOURTEEN
SEMI-NORMALCY AND NEW CHALLENGES

I managed to keep our daily life comparatively stable through the first four of Erika's elementary school years. She went to class every day, continued gymnastics and piano lessons, and had regular sleepovers with her friends. The three of us welcomed overnight visitors when time, energy, and steadiness allowed us to be congenial hosts. When Erika was in third grade, Oskar was asked to join the finance committee at our church, and I became the coordinator of children's programs.

One afternoon during the spring of 1975, we listed "family projects" we could do together. Erika and I bought tulip bulbs and red columbine seeds, and Oskar helped us plant them around the perimeter of our front yard. To honor Brian, we sowed a border of sunflower seeds along the uphill side of our back deck. Every time our son had grinned at the huge stalks in someone's garden, he called them "sunshine flowers." Eager to help the seeds become colorful beauties, we each took a turn at watering. There were days when I thought the plants might rot from too much moisture, but they thrived.

We had bought the lot next to us and, that same spring, decided to turn the front part without trees into a vegetable garden. First, we pulled blackberry vines and chopped out weeds. After tilling the compost and soil, we planted seeds for carrots, peppers, pumpkins, zucchini, spinach, and squash, with the tomato vines set to stakes. Erika watered the plants daily, and we all pulled weeds. When the shoots started breaking through, we toasted the coming bounty with root beer floats. Pempa barked to keep the deer away, and the vegetables grew into delicious summer salads and stir-fries.

We all loved the dog. With no dog parks, we took him for walks and runs in our neighborhood and let him roam our woods from a long tether. He seemed to enjoy all contact with us. But by his second summer, he had escaped several times. Erika and I made a plan to walk him twice daily, but some days, we couldn't avoid leaving home early in the morning and returning at dinnertime. Homework and household chores had to be fitted in, and on those days, Pempa got only short walks. We kept apologizing to him for missing his favorite sniffing and running opportunities.

Amid regrets and a lot of tears, we decided to seek a country home for him. Fortunately, a retired couple with a farm loved him instantly and promised long daily walks as well as dashes across a fenced portion of their property. The couple sent us photos of Pempa chasing rabbits and napping next to a baby lamb. Erika clearly missed her pet but was also happy for him. We sent a photo of her climbing trees and snuggling with Sunny.

In the years before Austria, Oskar and I enjoyed couple's getaways to resorts and ski lodges and road trips along the coast. Since the accident, my husband didn't even consider a night out for dinner and theater or a day trip as a twosome. I wondered if he was worried that his grief would show and that I would pick up on his discomfort and try to help him release it.

Although I believed he loved me, did he understand that I had tried very hard to make my devotion real by being strong for him? I questioned what he still valued about me. Did he see that I had to work at being extra organized and efficient so the household part of our relationship didn't collapse? And that I avoided burdening him with the details of my grieving, knowing it would add to his distress?

The internal burdens he continued to carry as the months and years passed appeared to sabotage his ability to feel and show even basic care and love for himself and others.

On a March Saturday in 1976, our new pastor stood at the door of the church and reached for Oskar's hand. He personally invited him to a men's retreat at a forested lodge the next weekend, saying it would be a great opportunity for time in nature and bonding with caring men. My husband took his hand back and rubbed his forehead, then blinked and blinked. He said, "I can't go," and walked to the car.

Erika wanted suggestions for whom to interview for her fourth-grade community and state project. I suggested she ask her dad, since he worked with the city and county. That evening, when he had turned over the last page of the local newspaper, she said, "Dad, what do you think should be three goals for our downtown area?"

"I have no idea," he said, furrowing his brow and staring at her, the paper plopped on the floor.

Erika stiffened. Later, I asked my husband if he realized how much his little girl just wanted to be close to him. Looking at his feet, he only replied, "Yes."

The small gestures of healing I took away from my neighbor's barberry bush and talks with women friends and Pastor Dan worked for many goals of my life but were much less effective when it came to issues that involved Oskar's relationship with his daughter. I often wanted to ask him, "What don't you get about embracing Erika's academic efforts or acknowledging her evolving friendships?" He didn't seem to understand how desperately she was attempting to achieve normalcy.

He couldn't give me a thumbs-up when I excitedly told him about students learning to read.

My teaching job, although rewarding, along with organizing our household amid family tensions, depleted my energy reserve. One April evening, I went to bed at seven o'clock but woke at two o'clock in the morning, the bed empty beside me. The light was still on in Oskar's office, and I stood in the doorway watching him sip coffee and stare at a photograph of his parents. In a childhood shot of the three brothers a few inches away, the youngest brother, Per, who inherited Bestemor's happy demeanor, smiled and tilted his head toward the serious Oskar. Reflecting how both seriousness and humor have value, and knowing that Oskar used to have a lighter side, I said, "When you smile, you look a lot like Per."

Showing no reaction to either photo, he continued to fixate on his parents without moving. I took a step closer and waited to hear him say something. Finally, I patted his shoulder and walked away.

A week later, I watched my husband take a large picture of Brian as an eighteen-month-old off the living room wall. The photo, with my son's quizzical expression, was a family favorite. Oskar left Erika's photograph in place and carried Brian's down to his office, avoiding my eyes. I replaced the picture that same day with another of my daughter, but he soon took that down, too. I found both behind his file cabinet. When I asked him if he wanted to choose a different photo—of anything or anyone, he looked down and said nothing. I could only think he felt the empty space was sacred.

One evening when Erika and I were reading together on the sofa, Oskar sat down in his blue chair, opened his book about the US Civil

War to the middle, and started to read. He quickly closed it and, for long minutes, focused his eyes on the front windows. Finally, Erika said, "Is that a boring book, Dad?" He blinked and walked up to our bedroom.

When I came to bed, the lights were out and the book lay closed over his chest. I set it on the nightstand and never saw him open it again. Maybe it was boring, but perhaps an idea had triggered a bad memory. The same demeanor played out again and again and in other ways: he discarded gifts with photos or paintings of children, avoided movies with young people as characters, and continued his silence. He had always been taciturn, but now he appeared determined to avoid all emotion.

Days after the book incident, I watched Oskar set his finished plate aside and point to his daughter's untouched serving of broccoli. He told her to eat it. The next night, Erika asked to be excused before she had tasted her peas and carrots. He said, "You can leave."

I didn't believe his comments had anything to do with his own or Erika's like or dislike of certain vegetables—or whether they were good for his daughter. His curtness was coming from something deeper, and I felt caught between my daughter and my husband. Later that night when he walked downstairs to his office, I asked if he had a reason for letting Erika skip the vegetables. He looked at me and blinked. I took his arm and said, "We need to be on the same page regarding how to help Erika make good choices. How would you suggest we treat the vegetables in her meals?" He stood and faced me without blinking until I backed out the door. When he closed it, pictures rattled in the hall.

I mostly served Erika vegetables she readily ate, with "tasting amounts" of those she didn't. She eyed me, seeming to understand I had a different goal than her father. A few times, she played me against him and said he would let her leave her green beans.

It became more difficult to hold my anger about Oskar's parenting inconsistencies, and one night at the dinner table, I said to
Erika in a loud voice, "You and I will decide about vegetables and
portions, not your father." She burst into tears, and Erika and I had
to decompress for an hour. We agreed that her father was unable to
think clearly right now and we should give him space. I hated that we
weren't addressing the root issues.

Anger over Oskar's inability to honor Erika's and my attempts
to move forward drove me to release frustrations by banging the
vacuum up and down the steps at eight o'clock at night or slamming
plates into the dishwasher without rinsing them. Oskar never asked
me what was wrong, and when I stopped vacuuming to look at him,
he shrugged and walked stiffly away.

There were times when I started to raise my voice at him, but
when I saw Erika's expression or knew she was nearby, I stopped,
often retreating to walk outside in the dark. My eyes raised toward
the heavens, I asked for wisdom and support to let the anger go. Often
when an issue overwhelmed me, I closed myself in a bathroom and
cried. Sometimes, I twisted and pulled at a washcloth until it ripped.

It was becoming clear that my husband's guilt and inability to cope
with Brian's memory, combined with life's stresses, were propelling
him into the depths of despair. His younger brother, Doug and Gayle,
as well as Pastor Dan saw his diminished contact with everyone as
a deepening refusal to come to terms with Brian's death—and with
the people related to it. I invited Oskar to join me for a short series of
counseling sessions, but he again said no.

Family and friends cared, but everyone had tried in every way
they knew to help him not give up on himself and to seek a path
where he could deal with the loss. I had believed that if he faced his

despondency on even a limited and surface level, a measure of relief would come. I saw slivers of openness grow over time when I tried that for myself.

Could Oskar process his own grief now or ever? I didn't know.

I continued to ignore my own mental suffering and constantly repeated words to stay balanced and normal for Erika and my students—while my husband's distance and resistance increased my feelings of detachment and confusion. What saved me was prayer and my mother's conviction that each iris plant is a living being with a unique purpose. Although Oskar frustrated and angered me, I had to let him play out his life—seemingly without input and help from me or anyone.

What had Brian's life meant to me? Fearing I would forget his special qualities, I decided to find a new memory of him every day and invite Erika to share one of her own. Those moments brought joy to each of us.

One evening in mid-spring, I fell into bed by myself and called Brian's cat, Sunny. He jumped to my side, touched his wet nose to my cheek, and licked it. Settled on my chest, he relaxed me with his soft purring. I wondered if Oskar would ever kiss me again, let alone sleep close to me.

I woke up at three o'clock in the morning to find the cat gone and my husband at the far edge of our king-sized bed, facing the wall. I felt more alone than at any time since we left Austria. At breakfast, Oskar got up after two swallows of coffee, gave Erika and me a barely audible "Bye," and headed out the door.

More and more episodes took place—from important decisions to the most mundane events—where he refused to engage in any way. Investing money, a parent conference, or fixing a leaky faucet—all carried the same weight of silence. I had to measure my words care-fully when I asked whether he was completing important household routines such as bill paying or monitoring investments. When a heavy chair he decided to return sat tied down inside his trunk for two weeks, I finally wrestled it out and fit it into mine. He asked me what I was doing. "I am taking it back," I said.

The environment Oskar and I had nurtured for our children had altered dramatically, leaching contentment from three lives. The void raised my level of anxiety about where we were headed. I worked harder every day to find creative ways to keep the lid on the sim-mering pot. Erika's apparent stable and sanguine growth served as a comfort. Advised to find specific tasks each day to keep us both physically and mentally busy, I used necessary routines as a game. Cutting cucumber slices to look like flowers and folding towels into animal shapes challenged us to the point of laughter.

I often took walks in our woods to clear my brain and think about how I had tried to partner with Oskar in recovery. When I sensed a rare instance in which he was approachable, I took his hand or patted his shoulder. I tucked "I love you" notes into his pockets and brief-case. But could I have missed the key connection to his mind and heart? It is possible, but at this juncture, I didn't know what it was.

As time went on, I got more insight into his feelings of loss and isolation. Oskar was coping in the only way he knew.

But, like many parents, the loss of a child was driving us apart.

FIFTEEN
CHOOSING TO RESET

All spring, Erika talked about her crowded classroom and dreamed of a fifth grade with fewer students. I took a personal leave day at the end of April, and we visited a private school eight miles south of town. On the drive home, my daughter said she was impressed with the friendly kids, the library's collection of mythologies and autobiographies, and the multitude of science projects.

"They even had two copies of *The Little Prince*, and the soccer teams seemed to win every game." Her answer was a resounding *Yes!* to attending fifth grade there. I suggested that if we lived closer to the school, playing after-school sports and connecting with classmates would be easier.

A new learning environment for Erika and a different house in a fresh setting. A chance to update life goals for each of us and begin again. A big step, but one deserving serious consideration.

At dinner, Erika and I told Oskar about the school. In a barely audible voice and with his head bowed, he agreed it might be a good fit. When she left to do homework, I asked her father about buying property in that area. He studied my face, rubbed his eyes, and went to his office to think. The next morning at breakfast, he said I should look at listings, and days later, he agreed to come to a showing. He was late, with no explanation or apology, but appeared open to the property.

The following Monday, one of his colleagues handed him the address of a country home for sale a short distance from the school. It was on three acres with forest views from three decks. We made an offer, and I assured Erika she could invite friends for sleepovers. "Can I get Pempa back and paint my new room yellow?" she asked.

"Yes, and yes," I said.

I saw this as a step toward healing for each of us and hoped the new surroundings would bring an emotional perspective not considered or available before. Because Oskar accepted the plan, I prayed the quiet, natural surroundings and the absence of the familiar four walls would release memories that held him down. Could he start to face his issues with openness? That was my prayer. I looked forward to bolder steps on my personal path, and I know Erika did too.

In the middle of June 1976, I listed our house for sale, and by the next week, we had three full-price offers.

We stood in our living room and pondered what to sell or give away. The decisions were individual and difficult. Over the next few days, I watched how Oskar and Erika touched, smiled at, or frowned at the furniture, pictures, and other mainstays of our lives. We agreed that the living room set, family room furniture, and Brian's bedroom set would go to people who couldn't afford to buy them. With Oskar's blessing, my daughter and I also donated certain bookshelves and small tables that had given us their best use. The heirlooms and mementos posed harder choices.

Although I would have agreed to bring each of the inherited items from both families to the new house, Oskar wanted to sort the Norwegian pieces—the hand-decorated wooden furniture, needlework pillows, and original ski equipment our children learned on. At the final selection, he kept only a few items.

On the first packing day, the last week of July, I got up at dawn in the warm air to set empty boxes outside the bedrooms. Oskar met me in his pajamas at Brian's doorway, and we stood there together. His stiffness said, *I can't face the heart-wrenching memories right now.* He left to get dressed while I assembled tape, scissors, and marking pens.

Picking up the four cartons for Brian's room, I set one each in front of the dresser, desk, bookcase, and bed. The important symbols of his life—books, artwork, and cherished music—had kept him alive for me every time I held them close or talked about them. I felt that was true for Erika, also. Although she didn't say much about Brian's room, she read his books and studied his artwork.

Now I stood alone in the middle of the room, breathing in the slight citrus fragrance from resin on fir branches. I had placed them on the dresser to feel one last time how my son's woodland adventures inspired his drawings and paintings. His dress jacket, the one I talked him out of packing for Europe, hung in the closet as a sentinel to his resilience. I lifted it to my chest.

After breakfast, Oskar came slightly inside Brian's door with me. His sad eyes went to the desk and the small drawing book his son had tucked into his Europe suitcase to sketch plants, animals, and structures. The two of them had drawn our backyard plan in a similar sketchbook. With the same somber expression, my husband peered at the bed's coverlet, presumably not touched by him since before the trip. I asked if he wanted private time, but he shook his head and walked downstairs.

I sat on the bed and smoothed the coverlet's tiny cornflowers before folding it into the largest box. This made me think of how Brian and I loved to hang out in grassy areas and watch insects move their delicate legs over tiny flowers. When I picked up the recorder from the nightstand, it carried me back to evenings when I would pause outside the door and listen to my son play himself to sleep. I tucked the instrument into the coverlet with a reminder that I could play Beethoven's "Für Elise" or the Mexican folk song "De Colores" and recall a multitude of shared musical moments. The baseball mitt fit at the top of a clothes box, and I stood his bat beside the box.

Holding the troll dolls close, I carried them from the hobby room, wrapped three layers of tissue around their bodies, and settled them above his framed spaceship and ocean liner drawings. I gently laid the photo of the four of us beside the trolls, folding my hands to the images.

On the top and side of the boxes, I wrote TREASURES FROM BRIAN. KEEP CLOSE. I would store them in my new office until it felt right for Erika and me, or just me, to unpack them. Since Brian's loving, courageous personality shone through every one of the keepsakes, I saw them as a healing tool and arranged the boxes carefully in my car.

Later, my daughter knelt at her brother's bookshelf and placed titles inside a box. Then she picked up *Banner in the Sky* and read the last page, doing the same for *The Secret Garden*, *Charlotte's Web*, and *Beezus and Ramona*. She packed all our favorites in two boxes and labeled them: READ AGAIN. *Henry Huggins*, still a favorite of mine today, lay across the top of the last shelf to pack. She said, "Henry was kind like Brian." She must have brought it to her brother's room. Erika crammed her too-small hat from the California Skunk Train trip into a box and set Brian's larger one on her head.

The dining room table and its chairs, brimming with memories of happy meals, were loaded into the van. Since Oskar chose not to offer an opinion, I decided to keep our bedroom furniture, hoping it would bring reminders of happier times. I packed and loaded our favorite board games.

When all the giveaway items had been claimed and our house was empty, Oskar closed the doors to the van. I wrapped my arms around my daughter and breathed in strength to link the memories of today—the pleasant, poignant, and sad—with the opportunities of tomorrow.

We gathered at the picnic table on our back deck for a final meal. I divided the leftover macaroni casserole into three portions and served it with a salad. Oskar tightened his lips and furrowed his brow, smoothing back his hair. Then he cut his macaroni into smaller bites, glanced several times at the side of the deck, and sprinkled a large amount of salt. He set his fork down, stared at his plate, and rubbed his eyes. After several minutes, he lifted his head and walked to the sunflower plants growing by our deck railing.

After touching a tall stalk, he came back, eyes downcast. I got up and put my arms around him. Erika said, "Maybe we can plant sunflowers at our new house." Later, she suggested that the plants would grow best in the dirt below the large living room window.

The "sunshine flower" promised to keep Brian with us in a loving way, and I promised myself I would plant seeds the next spring.

We had eaten our last bittersweet morsel when Sunny bounded up the deck steps to be fed. Tummy full, he scurried to the front entrance and, from his haunches, pawed at the door.

He seemed to say, *Let's get going to our new home.*

SIXTEEN

THE DIFFERENT VIEW

The new house sat several hundred feet below the road, and tall evergreens spread across the sloping back acreage, like our former home. The side lawn was large enough for a baseball game, with sunny space for a garden nearby. We had decided we could live without a creek and would petition for city water in the future.

Erika loved her new room's August Moon wall color and showed Oskar and me exactly where to place her bed, dresser, and desk. After I helped her hang her clothes, she unpacked books at record speed, eager to get organized for a sleepover with Robin and Marnie. *And*, her expression told me, *I want to do this by myself.* When I asked her what she liked best about the sprawling digs, she named her room, the decks, and new woods to explore. She also shared her excitement for school to start, almost echoing Sunny's, *Let's get on with it.*

Interior remodelers finished gluing grass cloth to a living room wall and set down the last pieces of updated floor treatments and kitchen counters. We arranged our new living room furniture, including the soft-pillowed burgundy sofa and matching chairs. The second evening, Erika dug into books she had read with Brian and asked to curl up with me for *The Secret Garden*. She planned to write down the names of the plants and flowers and find out if our extensive back property contained any of the varieties.

Oskar weighed in strongly regarding which of Brian's items

should be displayed. Other than the troll dolls and our son's recorder, which went to the family room bookshelf, all memorabilia went to Erika's room or my office. I wasn't sure what my husband's preferences were with the family photos, including sets of parents and grandparents. I set the boxes in the middle of the family room and invited him to help decide what we should hang. He took out the framed pictures of both of our parents and set them beside the baby pictures of Brian and Erika. He began hanging the baby photos with one parent couple on each side. Later, he sorted through a box of snapshots of the four of us, choosing final selections from our children's first five years. I attached the pictures Oskar approved to a medium-sized board and hung it on the wall at the end of the room. Photo albums from after the accident to the present stayed on a bottom bookshelf.

The collage from the hallway at our former house, spanning Brian's birth to just before the European trip, as well as the "together forever" photo of the four of us taken the fall before Europe, went to my office. I never saw Oskar look at either, and I can only assume he agreed to the family room display because he had hand-selected every photo.

My daughter didn't hesitate to say what she believed we should do with an item belonging to her brother. His baseball mitt and, of course, the train hats found a permanent place in her room, along with the blue-striped shirt and Rocky Bear. Most titles from the two boxes of "Read Again" books from Brian's room went to her bookcase, and photos from several family adventures lived at the center of her desk.

Erika and I bought a curved corner shelf unit for my office and placed the cornflower bedspread, a few of Brian's books, his sheet music, and the maple seed helicopter there. I hung his drawing of the big ship cruising downriver next to my desk. The "together forever" photo leaned against the front of the reading lamp, with two packets of sunflower seeds at its back.

I had entertained the idea of recreating Brian's room, but my son was gone. The best Erika and I could do was to be a part of his treasures, remembering the contribution his books, drawings, music, and sports equipment made to his life and ours.

The first fall days, when we sat down to meals at our new butcher-block breakfast table, Oskar gave his traditional *takk for maten* thank-you. I was pleased to see him express gratitude. Once in a while, in our cozy bedroom with its knotty alder ceiling and deep pile carpet, he would tell me in as few words as possible that he liked my egg and cheese quiches and omelets. Sometimes he half-smiled at me when we settled into bed with books. Falling asleep with the pages over his nose was still his preferred way of saying good night.

On a snowy January evening, the first winter in the new house, flames shimmered inside the circular glass fireplace as the three of us played Chinese checkers. Erika moved her green marbles to the opposite side first and held up her hand for high fives. After three games, each of us had a win. The competition was friendly, and Oskar teased his daughter that he would be the grand winner next time. Playing checkers was part of my strategy for a family tradition we could reinvent.

It seemed that my husband was trying to engage in his own way and to view himself in a pragmatic light. I knew any semblance of inner peace would come in small steps. More often now, he opened up about household matters, occasionally supported getting together with friends, and helped plan trips for the three of us. I complimented his formal but caring overtures, which, to some extent, resembled his demeanor before the accident. On a trip to Cozumel and Mexico City the summer after the move, I got sick and wanted to sleep. Although Erika kept saying, "Mom's fine, let's go explore," the two only left for brief periods. I believe it was Oskar's way of showing love and care.

During the first three years at our country home, we again made family budgets together and worked in our yard on weekends. We bicycled on the San Juan Islands. We slept in our VW Westfalia camper on long drives to California and made the cross-country trip from Oregon to Maryland in three days and nights to attend a family wedding.

The camper's thick foam back seat folded down to make a comfortable standard bed. With sheets and soft blankets, Erika slept through the night as Oskar and I took turns driving the turnpikes or napping beside our daughter. I was set up with excellent highway maps and directions, so with bleary eyes at three in the morning, I could move us closer to the East Coast. Since Oskar had no problem staying awake during his night shifts, I could doze peacefully.

Although I couldn't know how my husband and daughter were handling their private struggles, I felt a degree of optimism that we all engaged with life and made the effort to support each other. The sunshine flower seeds I planted grew below the living room picture window and faced the large grass lawn. Sunny napped in their shade, and I believed he felt Brian's presence there.

I was able to focus on my daughter's academic enrichment and develop literature, writing, and science curricula for her and for my students. Hikes to collect multiple leaf species for collages excited both Erika and my fifth graders. My daughter and I explored bookstores and libraries to study mythology, and I designed a literature unit featuring Greek gods and goddesses. Erika and her girlfriends turned the stories into plays, as did my students.

It was a great relief for my mind and heart to be on a more normal path again. Oh, how I had missed it, but I didn't know to what degree until I could once again interact with children and adults without the multiple clouds of worry and apprehension.

During Erika's seventh-grade year, Oskar and I became counselors for the youth group at our church. She cajoled her dad into helping her learn to tie the bowline, clove hitch, and figure eight. She took him hiking on forest trails to look for raccoon, cougar, and bear tracks, moving her toward earning an animal-tracking badge. One afternoon after they returned from an outing, Erika hurried to find me.

"We saw foot pads under a blackberry vine with five toes and three claw marks. Up the trail, we found scat, probably black bear." I could see that occasions like these let her feel her father's love.

I said to Oskar, "I'm impressed that you've gotten your daughter excited over scat." He simpered, smoothing the sides of his hair.

As I looked back on the summer, I realized Oskar was less and less present. More importantly, he hadn't said one word about the accident or about Brian—or described his own feelings with even a few words. I attributed at least some of this to job stress, but by fall, Erika's eighth-grade year, Oskar's engagement with her and with me was clearly subsiding.

That winter, he again showed no interest in household routines and family appointments. By spring, he had often failed to pick Erika up from her piano lesson and came late for dinner without a reason or apology. Most nights, he sat in his office at the end of the hall until long past midnight. His job reassignment required additional skills and hours, but I often found him staring at pictures of his parents and his family. Something else was going on. When he came to bed on time, he was silent, his arms and legs stiff and close to his body.

He had added a new burden to his anguish, or the old ones had gone deeper.

I sought advice from our pastor, who believed Oskar's sense of failed duty had intensified. Suggesting I continue allowing wide space, he advised seeking counseling for us both. I interviewed several professionals and chose one, but after three sessions, I saw that she lacked experience in handling family-related grief issues. My husband stayed away. He also said no to another men's retreat and to visiting with our clergy friend. Not only did he never mention Brian, but it seemed he worked extra hard to keep the remotest connections off his radar. I had to believe it was becoming too painful for this "stalwart Norwegian" to see or hear his son's name, and no words, however delicately spoken, caused him to open up.

I was losing my husband. Again.

On a cold February evening, Erika and I sat close to the fireplace reading. I commented on the coziness of the yellow heat as Oskar added logs. Erika murmured, "It's so comfy," and watched her dad sit down near a distant wall. She closed her book, went to him, and said, "Can I talk to you about what Abraham Lincoln and Jimmy Carter have in common?" Her homeroom teacher, Mr. R, had challenged his students to compare the leadership styles of historical and modern politicians.

Oskar stiffened his lower lip over his upper, picked up his newspaper, and covered his face. Erika rubbed her eyes and waited. Finally, her father said, "Maybe Mr. R can tell you."

I followed my daughter out of the room. We sat arm in arm, our faces serious. After several minutes, she said, "I know Dad loves me, but when he ignores every question I ask, it really hurts."

I offered that his grief and pain over Brian caused him to say things he never would have said before the accident. I told her I would ask him what he had meant.

When I did, he said, "I can talk to Erika the way I want to."

That answer crushed me. How could he treat his lovely, talented, innocent daughter that way? His behavior toward her continued to be disturbing. One day, he told me she preferred Sandy, her classmate and neighbor, to him. I had a strong sense he wished I would tell him it was true and feel sorry for him. I couldn't, even though his confusion and struggle made my head and heart ache. Instead, I said, "Erika will never quit being your daughter and wanting your input and advice, even when it appears otherwise." I added that it was normal for kids as they got older to spend more time with friends while still loving and respecting their parents.

I began to understand how difficult managing deep sorrow can be. I hurt for both my husband and my daughter. Being so close to the issues, it was impossible to be objective, and I lacked real training and skills. When I tried to recharge my own spirit, the tapes of Oskar's actions replayed. Some days I wanted to stay in bed and let whatever happened happen. I prayed for wisdom.

During the summer break, Erika and I attended a spiritual retreat, camping for the week. It was inspiring for both of us, but after three days, I found my teen daughter spending more time in our tent reading than going hiking, swimming, or doing group activities with her peers. She seemed to have lost her zest, but she wouldn't tell me how she felt or what she wanted to do instead. My sister-in-law suggested I give Erika more attention and see if I could draw her out. I left my discussion groups, and for the rest of the week, we explored the nearby wild area together. She perked up and shared feelings about her father's growing reluctance to be part of her life. I felt her anxiety, tasted the bitterness, and told her I understood her need to bond with other people. I assured her I would never abandon her or her feelings about herself or her dad.

While we broke down camp, Oskar's issue about Erika suddenly became clear: *He couldn't bear to watch his only child grow up and away from him.* I told her that, in some ways, her dad's recent behavior showed how much he loved her—he felt he was losing his little girl to the world.

Although Oskar's issues with Erika were more complicated than separation anxiety, this matter had become embedded in his larger grief. I stayed awake nights running through additional reasons for his distancing behavior, and strategies or people with clues to a therapy that might reach him. None came.

What stopped me from confronting him further was that he would consider my words—whether reassuring or an effort to draw out his feelings—as "none of my business."

For some people, new environments add to loss instead of serving as an energy path. I saw Oskar as one of them.

I had to leave his struggles with God.

SEVENTEEN

A RIVER FORKS HARD RIGHT

Erika and I rode bikes in the fresh air, and we hiked trails and buttes. She took special care of her pansy plants and said, "Every flower has the prettiest face, eyes, and nose." The sunflowers continued to bloom.

Movement released the pent-up emotion we consistently developed. Erika also took karate and spent hours driving her new gas-powered scooter up and down our road. One spring day, her ninth-grade year, I brought my second graders to our home for a field trip, and she delighted in offering them short rides down the driveway. We saw hard work as an antidote to stress and washed windows and pulled weeds when we felt the need to decompress.

That summer, a counselor named Dick helped me look at Oskar's accelerating patterns of evenings spent at his office, ignoring household chores, and choosing not to join Erika, me, or friends for social events. Dick concurred that my husband's panic over watching his only child grow up was exacerbated by his guilt over not saving his son. Dick suggested I invite Oskar to come for a session with me or by himself. I made the offer but was met with refusal on both counts. The counselor's short-term recommendation was to be supportive during Oskar's efforts to connect. Erika thanked her father for helping cut dead branches, while I smiled in agreement when he quietly called a maple tree that grew between two firs *modig* (Norwegian for *brave*).

Although I was weary of constantly self-checking my strengths and competencies, I promised to keep my husband's issues from interfering with my role as Erika's mother and his role as her father. With that purpose, I begged him to talk about his concerns with a pastor or friend. He declined. Nothing helped him see he shouldn't interfere with his daughter's healthy friendships. Dick also counseled Erika and, considering our family's difficulties, felt she was handling life remarkably well. His advice to her was to walk quickly away when words or actions turned hurtful.

I needed an alternative professional challenge—one where I had more control over my work hours. A paid leave the following year let me develop a literature-based program for beginning readers. Its success told me that large numbers of children could benefit from the unique approach. I became a guest lecturer at a local university and led workshops for neighboring school districts. The revitalizing feelings enabled me to put home pressures at a different kind of distance and gave me an opportunity to process Oskar's increasing negativity without responding, trying to fix his issues, or blaming myself.

Erika's attempts to tell her father how much her friends admired his longtime simple yet effective carpentry skills, his quick repair of a bike on the trail, and his strong swimming ability should have swelled his heart. But he was unable to grasp his own significant contribution to his extraordinary children. For many years, he had given his all, but now he seemed unable to see his daughter for the magnificent person she was or to acknowledge his role in her ability to thrive.

I never gave up advocating for and with Oskar because I had always believed—and continued to maintain—that two parents, however flawed, are better than one. I worked to keep myself well-grounded for Erika. My daughter would graduate from high school in three years and launch an independent life. When she showed off her diploma, I wanted to affirm, "Erika's physical, emotional, and spiritual needs came first." That goal kept me from being preoccupied by my own.

Snowflakes curtained the VW station wagon's windows as Oskar drove us through the Cascade Mountains to Central Oregon. Our daughter and her friend Pam, now tenth graders, enticed me to estimate the number of ice crystals that fell in ten seconds and then try to count them. When we arrived at our Sun River Resort cabin, all was forgotten except five days of skiing at Mount Bachelor.

The evening before we headed home, I became concerned about the report of icy conditions on the passes. The Davis Lake route was forecasted to be clear by early afternoon, and we decided to try it. The sun radiated through the trees as we drove beside banks of snow piled several feet high. Stopping at the top of the pass, surrounded by a pristine white expanse, I took deep breaths of the crisp air. What I could see of the road appeared dry and clear.

We had driven this route other times in the same road conditions. I was a slower, more cautious driver, especially on mountain roads. Experience had taught me that if small patches of ice hadn't melted, the road could be dangerous. Oskar always drove close to the allowed limit but at a safe speed. He was usually at the wheel when our family went on outings.

Although I couldn't figure out why, I felt uneasy about his driving today. When he started the engine for the winding downward journey through tall trees, I faced him and said, "Please drive slowly— very slowly." He nodded.

I glanced at my husband continuously as we motored toward the first curve. The road became more shaded and narrower with each bend. At the first sharp corner, when my arm hit the side of Oskar's seat, I grabbed his shoulder and said, "Slow down." He reduced the speed somewhat, but the next curve was steeper, and the car swerved enough for me to yell, "Slow down now!"

His speed around the third curve, another left, was again too fast for the conditions, and I cried out, "Pull over!" He couldn't, and the car suddenly fishtailed across the center and back, headed left, and picked up speed. He corrected to the right, and the car skidded into the packed bank and jumped several feet. I screamed to the girls, "Hold on tight." Rotating toward my side, the VW kept turning and flipped, the roof landing on the snow. My legs dangled toward the ceiling, and my head grazed the floor. I felt the wheels spin as they pointed at the sky.

I twisted sideways to verify that the girls were okay.

Erika and Pam were silently huddled together behind us. I asked them to talk to me, and they did. I didn't remember what happened beyond that until I stood in the snow, my arms hugging both girls tightly. We all felt overwhelming joy that no one was hurt. It was clear that a shaded area contained patches of black ice that the sand truck had missed, and our wheels had hit one or more, spinning out of control. A helpless feeling overtook my chilled body.

I was deeply worried about my husband. After our friends who had followed us got us settled in their car, regret filled me. Something had caused Oskar to disregard caution. I suspected he had been drinking alcohol. Why had I let him drive?

When I had questioned his possible drinking on other occasions, I managed to find extraneous reasons—or simply excuses—for his behavior.

I tossed and turned for several nights, believing more firmly with every detailed recounting that alcohol had led to the recklessness.

Before we left the bedroom five mornings after the rollover, I asked Oskar what had kept him from driving more slowly when he knew that ice spots were a potential hazard. He blinked and looked away.

I said, "Do you realize your fast driving was irresponsible under those conditions—and could have cost our daughter, her friend, and you and me our lives?" He walked toward the door and said nothing. I also told him that I didn't believe he meant to be reckless.

Again, I said, "What caused you to drive out of control?"

He looked away, totally silent.

When we lost Brian, Oskar and I had made a joint, conscious choice to help Erika enjoy a long, happy life. He had jeopardized this resolve. I hoped that our near-disaster would be a serious enough wake-up call to prompt him to seek help. Erika and Pam seemed to have taken the rollover in stride, joking about it several times. When I continued to ask my daughter whether she was really okay with her feelings, she kept insisting she was.

Over the following weeks, my husband spent hours resharpening tools in the garage, piling up dead branches from the reaches of property we never walked through, and creating multiple expenditure grids for household expenses. At meals and whenever he was near Erika or me, he avoided our eyes, pursed his lips when he didn't have to talk or eat, and if he had to engage, flipped his mouth up and down from smile to frown and frown to smile. His arms were often crossed.

I decided to pay even closer attention to his behavior and personal habits and relieved him of the duties of picking Erika up after school and from karate. When the three of us drove somewhere, I insisted on being at the wheel. During that late winter and spring, when we invited friends for dinner or table game evenings, Oskar repeated stories and anecdotes, a behavior out of character for him. One evening in May, I was alarmed when he grinned at the end of a friend's tragic story.

I prayed and hoped beyond hope that he was staying sober for his day job while I figured out what to do.

In hindsight, I should have realized sooner that Oskar had a drinking problem and actively addressed the issue—although my gut told me at every juncture that he would never have admitted to regularly consuming large amounts of alcohol. Presentations for his company during the first years of our marriage stressed him, and I knew he had infrequently taken a colleague's suggestion of a shot of gin. His more conservative religious roots didn't condone consuming alcohol, and I had for a long time trusted that the occasion for his drinking was to pacify his anxiety for work-related speaking engagements.

At the very least, I had been lulled into thinking Oskar drank responsibly. The reality was that he went to great lengths to hide his drinking habit.

I had always believed that an occasional glass of beer or wine with my girlfriends was a positive lifestyle choice. I never drank with Oskar and considered myself fortunate that alcohol never was anything close to an addictive disorder for me.

For a while, Oskar's secret was at least somewhat hidden.

I now understood his drinking had become a part of who he was.

The decision: when and how to confront him.

The next week, I watched him stumble down the three steps to our living room. Soon after, I cleaned up our hobby room off the garage and discovered two empty vodka bottles in a holiday decorations crate. I sat beside him at his desk and lifted the bottles out of the bag. "Can you tell me about these?"

He glanced at me and then looked down at the papers on his desk.

"I was in a hurry, so I just dropped them into a crate," he said.

I took a breath, and said, "Okay. And are you a regular, copious drinker?"

He told me he drank when he wanted to. When I asked him if that was every day, he said nothing. Soon after, he refused to give me the keys to the trunk of his car.

How long had Oskar been drinking? And how regularly? I was sure that Erika's friendships outside the family, coupled with guilt over the tragedy, had caused him to reach a boiling point, and he believed he could only survive with enough alcohol to numb the pain. Looking back, I believed it had become an unmanageable habit more than two years earlier. His family's literal adherence to biblical principles was not enough to keep him from drowning his grief and guilt.

I needed more information about alcohol addiction. Now.

The next week, I went to an Al-Anon meeting so I could learn the details of this substance abuse. Al-Anon is a fellowship for family and friends who advocate for and support an alcoholic's recovery. The message is that although others can be supportive, the real work must be done by the drinker himself. I wondered if Oskar would ever be willing to go to an AA meeting or to a counselor. He appeared resolute that he had the right to behave as he chose. When his past decisions addressed his conservative heritage in a realistic way, I could understand.

Now, he stubbornly insisted he had the right to privacy as he destroyed his bedrock relationships. His behavior wasn't just his business. Besides his own sobriety, the welfare of our family—including his job—was at stake. I invited him to seek help with AA.

I pleaded with him to consider therapy. *For all our sakes.* Nothing I said—or didn't say—convinced him to admit that his drinking created another hurdle for Erika and me.

EIGHTEEN
COPING

Preparing and practicing for the Fourth of July annual local marathon got me stretching and running two or three miles most afternoons and five miles on weekends. I pumped away tension along back roads with fields of cows grazing nearby. I could relax for a few minutes afterward. On the Sunday of the race, my goal was to finish the twenty-six miles in a comfortable time. I did, and I felt "a stream of accomplishment" as my daughter poured water over my head. Oskar stood nearby and tried to smile—a rare moment.

At least partially aware of the risk to his job, he appeared to keep the alcohol under control during the workday. Taking frequent showers, wearing clean clothes, and using liberal amounts of mouthwash seemed to let him avoid being identified with alcohol addiction, now called Alcohol Use Disorder. Only occasionally did his breath have telltale odors. It wasn't that Oskar never engaged with us, but the times he was mentally and spiritually present in even a casual way were becoming rarer and felt less genuine.

Every fiber of my being wanted to spare Erika possible angst. My pain from this, combined with my commitment to clarity about Oskar's effect on his daughter, prompted me to wait for the right opportunity for a serious talk with her about his drinking.

In retrospect, I know that children often perceive and are willing to face alcohol-related issues before adults. The day after the marathon, I sat down for a heart-to-heart with Erika and asked her if she would share some recent feelings about her dad.

She was silent for several minutes, and then she said, "Mom, I know Dad drinks a lot of alcohol." She told me that he occasionally behaved like a friend's grandfather, who slurred his words and forgot to show up for family gatherings. She assured me she loved her father, even though lately it was hard to feel like he cared about her.

We shared the ways we had both tried to bolster Oskar's self-image and assure him of our love. I told Erika that whether or not her father got help with his drinking, she could count on me. I assured her that when she wanted to talk, I would drop everything and listen. Revisiting my awareness of Erika's needs that lurked under the surface, I promised myself to be more vigilant to her subtle stressors.

My hands grasping hers, I emphasized that her dad's drinking was in no way her fault or her responsibility to fix. "There is nothing for you to feel guilty about," I said and offered a prayer for loving herself and God. I repeated that I believed she had survived because she happened to be closer to the bank, and that it was in no way her fault we couldn't get to Brian. I told her that sometimes life defies explanation.

"Trust that you will see your brother again, and remember, he wants you to be happy today and forever," I said.

God gives us the breath of life and is beside us but doesn't make choices for individuals, the power company, or the natural world. Human response to nature's built-in systems is often imperfect and causes accidents to happen. Behind and beyond all of this lies spheres of mystery.

Oskar appeared to keep his commitment and loyalty to his job. On days when he chose to be evasive and secretive, we left him to himself.

Erika and I did go to church, and if he came and our pastor invited him for a private visit, the gist of his answer was that he was handling his own problems.

One late evening, while he polished his shoes, I knelt beside him and said, "The daughter whose life you saved is having to distance herself from the dad you are becoming."

He refolded the cloth and kept polishing.

I believed there was nothing else to say. I had already voiced everything I considered helpful.

It was clear to me that the most difficult rapid for a father to paddle out of is the loss of his son. So many turns and side channels to face before finally moving through the challenge.

My focus turned to getting Erika and myself through the next two years with as much grace and fortitude as possible. If Oskar chose to be part of our commitment, we would welcome him. If he didn't, Erika and I would increasingly depend on each other and our trusted resources. I prayed he would hold himself together enough to keep his position with this caring company. Otherwise, with only my teaching salary, we would likely be forced to move, altering our lives even more significantly.

I saw the loss of Oskar's emotional support as the big issue it was. And because the full realization descended on me like a diving drone, I walked around with uplifted hands, not knowing the next step. I worried that I didn't have the stamina for the sole responsibility of parenting until our daughter graduated. I also understood that putting my own grieving increasingly on hold jeopardized not only me but Erika.

I couldn't bear to look at photos of Brian or his beautiful, intricate drawings because I felt empty of joy and unable to cry. This is what it means to lose touch with oneself, a dangerous state. Viewing my present journey as paddling without a float plan, I found it difficult to stabilize myself. If Erika mentioned her brother, I faked an interest and a smile, but she knew my reaction wasn't real. I was a worry to myself and afraid of becoming the same to my daughter.

My close friends were beside me every moment, but there were only so many approaches that helped steady me. They took me to dinner, we went on walks, and we did fun projects with our children. Pam's family and Erika and I explored parts of Oregon none of us had seen.

As her father moved further and further away, Erika gravitated to attentive adults like Mr. R. Her mentors, including our counselor, Dick, all assured me Erika was handling her father's issues quite well.

Although in some ways still a child, she was on the cusp of adulthood. I decided to defer to the experts. It gave me pause that my child had insights and self-control I didn't.

In June, I detached and regrouped for a weekend trip with two teacher friends to the Ashland Shakespeare Festival's performance of *King Lear*. We stayed in a turn-of-the-century bed and breakfast, had scones and tea, and strolled the trails of Lithia Park. The morning after the performance, we drove to the summit of nearby Mt. Ashland and picked our way across the granite. On a windswept ledge, I balanced my two feet on separate spurs and watched the Shasta red firs and mountain hemlocks sway below. I thought about how King Lear at first passed over his youngest daughter, Cordelia, and her love for him. I saw how personal tragedy begets more tragedy and chose to believe that the daughter stood for principle—her father finally seeing love as the answer.

One warm Sunday afternoon in early September of Erika's senior year, she cut the grass with the riding mower while I pulled weeds around the azaleas and rhododendrons. Oskar had gone to his office in town. Brian's cat, Sunny, and Erika's recently acquired cat, Swift Arrow, slept under the sunflower stalks. The vet had told me months ago that the yellow cat's arthritis had gotten worse, and I knew he was suffering, but I had hesitated to have him euthanized. The next day, I pulled into the carport and scanned the area for the cats. Swift Arrow came running, but Sunny didn't. We never found a trace of him.

I configured a cross from two branches, set it in front of his outlined shape under the sunflowers, and placed a ceramic cat planter with daisies on the form. I knelt and folded my hands, remembering how Sunny used to follow Brian to the creek at our former home, climb trees with him, and purr on his pillow. When I held him, I, too, was privy to his unique *purr-pause, purr-roar-pause* way of loving. We always kissed by touching noses like he did with Brian and with Erika.

I finally understood what Sunny had long favored: a bond with our family not unlike the one my son had with the three of us— uplifting, nonjudgmental, and soothing.

He stayed as long as he could to help us appreciate caring as part of truth.

NINETEEN
HALF A CELEBRATION

It was mid-October, and plans for Erika's spring graduation revived me. We brainstormed ideas about the reception and, with Oskar's input, decided to have it at our home. Sandy had gotten Erika interested in the senior photos and how each girl's hair would look after the cap came off. I was pleased she could focus on positive nitty-gritty details.

Exhausted but needing time beyond my surroundings, I decided to teach a four-hour class the next week at a community college fifty miles down the freeway. I was energized at the thought of literally driving away from the daily pressures to help new teachers plan curriculum programs. Oskar was gone more than he was at home, and Erika was delighted to spend some evenings with Sandy's family.

On the trip home, I stopped at a restaurant for a relaxing glass of wine and a dinner that fed me on all levels. The next day, I could again handle Erika's needs, my job, Oskar, the house, and sometimes my girlfriends. Although I was troubled on a level I had never experienced, I was finding ways to keep from giving up. This type of self-intervention allowed the mindset to parent, fit in some exercise, and steal a few hours for rest. On days the above routines broke down, I looked for small pleasures to carry me, such as a giggle from Erika, a quiet moment, or an unexpected blooming flower.

Once again, I invited Oskar to come to counseling. He agreed to go the next week. At the session, I faced my husband and told him I felt supported when he participated with us as a family but felt abandoned and troubled the many times he didn't. I said, "I sometimes can't help taking my frustrations out on Erika, which she doesn't deserve." When Dick asked for input from Oskar, he smoothed his eyebrows, pursed his lips, and simply said, "Erika is okay." After that session, he ignored all resources for help. By December, he was away until midnight most workdays. He repeatedly told me his job was keeping him busy beyond the normal workday, but knowing his company's reputation, I didn't believe him. When he was home, he hardly joined us on any level, and from the pain he must have been experiencing, it certainly would have been difficult.

Erika stiffened and was quieter when her father was around. When the two of us were alone, I sometimes asked her how she was coping. "I'm fine," she would say. If I probed further, she described the pain in watching her father isolate himself from enjoyment, silently fight misery, and not really get the nuances of anything she told him. My stomach churned, but we talked about ways she could move through this time by acknowledging both happy and sad feelings. She told me about what truly bothered her and that she talked to God privately. We asked each other, "What would Brian say?" already knowing his message: "Find moments that make you clap and be thankful for each one."

Erika shared examples of what made her clap. "Swift Arrow [her gray cat with the white arrow on his head] sneezes three times after he rubs my nose," and "My joke about the neighbors in the big 'battleship house' only living in two rooms makes Sandy laugh." Accepted into the local university's business school, my daughter would continue to live at our house and enjoy the cat and the neighbors for at least a short time.

In mid-December, I sought Dick's advice about asking Oskar to find an apartment after the holidays—hoping distance and privacy might give him some perspective. The counselor agreed that a temporary move could possibly restore a more positive context to Oskar's life. When I ran the idea by him, he just looked at me and walked away.

I decided to make the holiday season as special and upbeat as possible. Erika and I got Oskar to help cut a tree from our back property and haul it to our living room. It fit perfectly under the vaulted ceiling in front of the tall window. We attached Erika's dough snowman ornament—painted white with a red scarf and eyes of real beads—and hung Brian's pinecone reindeer with pipe-cleaner antlers and mouth. The two of us giggled as we struggled to get a Popsicle stick star to stay straight at the top of the tree. Bestemor had crocheted twenty red hearts, and after we hung them, I bent my head and blessed our efforts.

This was Erika's last Christmas as a high schooler, and I yearned for it to be one she could cherish. I bought the plumpest turkey I could find, roasted it, and stirred extra butter into the mashed potatoes. She didn't like turkey dressing, so I baked cornbread and served it with jam and honey. At the end of my prayer, I challenged us all to look to light and hope, ignoring Oskar's shaking hands and his silence. My daughter and I had to be satisfied that the three of us were opening presents together, eating at the same table, and staying warm beside the snapping logs in our fireplace.

On a cold night in early January, when I was about to remind Oskar to find an apartment, something happened that led to his acknowledgment of where his pain and guilt had led him. I was awakened at two o'clock in the morning by unusual noises in the garage. Glancing at the empty side of the bed, I hoped I wouldn't be confronting an intruder.

Flashlight and the dowel from a sliding door in hand, I walked through the dark hallway up the stairs to the garage door. Gripping the doorknob, I turned it slightly and listened. Nothing.

Peeking through the entrance, I shone the light at my husband's parking space. The car crackled from being recently driven but was unoccupied. I pushed forward to the sliver of brightness coming from the nearby hobby room and swung open the door to see Oskar sprawled face down on the cement floor. I shook him. He moaned and covered his head. I turned the switch off and went back to bed, tossing and clutching my stomach until five o'clock.

At the breakfast table, when I looked into Oskar's eyes, he bent his head, then told Erika and me he couldn't stop drinking and didn't want to seek help. "It gets me through the day," he said. "I'm going to look for an apartment."

Erika said, "If you get help, you *can* stop."

He walked out the door to his car.

My goal was to get my daughter and myself through the days until Oskar left with as much dignity as possible. Although I didn't voice it to him or to anyone, it was hard to see purpose or a favorable outcome for us as a couple after her graduation.

The days before Oskar's departure were tense. I tried to get through normal routines with as much finesse as I could muster, but my daughter's looks told me I was working too hard at being cheerful. While he packed up, I fertilized the rhododendrons and hacked at grass growing into the flower beds. Erika read and played music in her room while her father removed items from his home desk. After he pulled out of the driveway, she quietly closed his office door, then escaped to watch *Ghostbusters*, giggling into the night.

After Oskar moved into a studio, I thought I would feel relief and calm. I didn't. I felt responsible for everything and worried constantly that my daughter would see me as a failed mother. I kept wondering if I could have done something differently to stave off this final downturn. Dick, my pastor, my family, and my friends all assured me I couldn't have and reminded me of the energy and effort I had expended. On occasion, I dismissed their reassurances and blamed myself for having missed some critical moment to make a difference.

I found myself engaging in uncharacteristic acts of mischief to deal with the pressures. In early February, on an overcast night, I left Erika to do her homework and got into my car carrying twenty rolls of toilet paper. I met a teenage friend to TP the bushes and yard of a family who had played a prank on us. We worked until the paper ran out. Without a drop of alcohol, I laughed uproariously. A few evenings later, I drove to the house of a teetotaling couple, carrying a bottle of wine. I knocked at the door disguised in a white robe, crown, and mask as the Greek goddess Dionysus. I said, "I'm the bearer of grapes and drink. Where's the party?"

Although embarrassment came later, the pranks felt therapeutic. I did apologize for the large amount of toilet paper the family had to remove—and to the couple, although their son thought the wine was an apropos sentiment.

In April, I got called for jury duty. The short break in my schedule was a blessing that allowed me to revisit my efforts to be Erika's mother. I had demons knocking me down just as Oskar did: my own grief, guilt, and self-doubt. The difference was that I remained sober and forced myself to keep getting up and journeying onwards.

Every day was full in the final two months of school. The grass grew tall, but I had no time to cut it. I let clutter and dust pile up in the house with no hours to put things away or vacuum. I tried to stop leaks I had no skill for. Often, after my daughter and I had a quick dinner of warmed pizza, I collapsed in a chair, staying there until morning. I had school events to help Erika plan and my own job to keep afloat. Oskar ate with us once every week or two in a tense, short meal, collaborated with me on paying bills, and did a bit of yard work. We only saw him occasionally between those times. He didn't call, and this being a decade before cell phones, I had to drive around town to find his car in order to talk to him. Our conversations were brief and strictly business.

Thinking back today, I should have hired a housekeeper and a yard care person, but in the 1980s, families did this work themselves. At the time, I was the mom who did it all.

To say that I regretted not being able to fully enjoy the final months of my daughter's high school experience is an understatement. I was reassured by Erika's growing self-reliance and was eager to watch her stretch out to the world. But I longed for a partner to share this time with as well as to mourn the empty nest.

Erika's high school graduation was in two weeks. She and I had decided to honor Oskar's request for carrot and pea salad open-faced sandwiches, as well as my daughter's must-haves of ants on a log and yellow cheese on crackers. Then, three days before the ceremony, the last Thursday of May 1984, I bolted from bed and ran upstairs to the kitchen phone. I had forgotten to order the cake for Sunday's party. I dialed my favorite bakery. When the number rang and rang, I glanced at the clock. It read 6:30 a.m. I hung up, sat down, and dropped my head to the table where the to-do list lay under my arm. Moments later, Erika stood by my side and read item number one.

"It's okay, Mom; I can call about the cake."

I was determined that everything else I had promised to do would get done. Saturday evening, I set up a long table on our covered deck, spread a white cloth with blue trim, and positioned the party tableware.

Sunday morning, I made the finger sandwiches, including some with salmon, arranged the crackers, and filled celery with peanut butter. I was proud of my last-minute contributions, but when Erika joined me, her face said she didn't trust that I had gotten everything together. I hardly trusted myself.

By nine o'clock, when Oskar arrived, dressed in a blue suit, the sun illuminated the blooming rhododendrons bordering our lawns. I looked to the distant woods, took a long breath, and thought about Erika's intention to study for a business degree. She was young but tenacious, in many ways able to guide herself, and for her to be at a distance from her parents' struggles would give objectivity to her path. I prayed she would cede her parents' issues to the universe and to God, where they belonged.

That didn't mean she was free of issues—as the survivor of a tragedy, there are always grounds for reprocessing her growing-up years. But she had trustworthy friends and mentors, and she was disciplined and smart with goals I was confident she would achieve. I saw her gleaming nod to the future as her father and I watched her march across the platform and receive her diploma.

Our daughter had graduated. Even though we would all live separately, I promised to support and cheer her through college and beyond. Despite the years of turmoil, I had to believe I had done my best with this precious girl. And I could only hope she understood that. If he got treatment, Oskar had the opportunity to regain his important influence on her life.

My conviction that, as Oskar's partner, I had given everything I had made me sad. Not able to erase the person either he or I had become, we couldn't live together. We had done our best to rise above the issues. And we both believed we had a better chance of recovery as single people. I would always ache for the companionship gone awry and the marriage we couldn't continue, but years later, I understood more deeply how issues like the death of a child can leave permanent scars on relationships and often can't be resolved through intervention on any level.

The day after the graduation, Oskar spoke the words, "We should get a divorce." My usual reaction to intense decisions is to say, "Let's think about it," but we had effectively done that many times over. I filed the papers and we agreed to sell the house.

At this beginning of another kind of grieving, I had to muster every ounce of courage to take new steps, one at a time.

My last backward glance at our country home took me to the beauty of Brian's "sunshine flowers."

I picked one flower and held the flowerhead close to my face. Energy flowed from its center and outward to the yellow petals.

Strength beckoned me forward.

TWENTY
RIPPLES OF UNDERSTANDING

At the end of August, two friends and I set the burgundy sofa from our country home against the long wall in my new apartment. The butcher-block table occupied the other end. After we placed my desk and file cabinets in the second bedroom, I helped carry the dressers inside and set up the king-sized bed. The room looked crowded and dark, so I visualized a light-colored spread, white decorative pillows, and a slim floor lamp.

The furniture settled, my friends left, and I leaned against one of the sofa pillows. It felt familiar, yet I couldn't stir memories of curling up with Erika or reading with Oskar. I bought sunflowers, arranged them in a vase, and set the large bouquet at the center of the table. Each yellow petal glistened through stems deep inside the vase. I promised to change the water often and renew the flowers' spirit as an ode to Brian.

A teacher friend offered me her cabin on the Oregon coast for the Halloween weekend, with a weather forecast of unusually warm and cloudless days. I invited two colleagues for a relaxing celebration. We arrived late Friday afternoon and, wearing shorts and tank tops, carved pumpkins on the deck. We designed and cut fancy features, and when dusk fell, we lit candles to highlight the interesting noses, cheeks, and eyebrows. As I gazed at the different figures and flames, I thought back to a Halloween when Erika finger-painted a pumpkin with tempera paint. Her finger formed star eyes and heart cheeks. The treasured time I spent as wife and mother seemed to serve as a welcome symbol for this weekend and future adventures.

I wasn't prepared for the cold winter, the rain, and the snow-covered streets. The moisture seeped into my pores and filled them with icicles of doubt. The weather shifts played on my emotions and caused them to peak in directions similar to the forecasts. On days when I could tap into the sun-bathed Halloween weekend, I invited teachers and other friends for afternoon tea or an evening meal. Grief still had a hold on me, and some days, it was hard even to call out to God. But I dreamed of gentle breezes and summer's warmth, reminding myself a bright season was around the bend.

The full-time job, helping Erika feel cared for, and adjustments to accommodate my new life took the school year to June. My daughter and a girlfriend lived at our home until we listed the property for sale at the beginning of April. They took classes, did homework, and, in the evening, enjoyed adapting my recipes to suit their young-adult tastes. Swift Arrow was a good companion. I had dinner with them often. Oskar, from all reports, lived mostly at his studio. The girls said they hardly saw him and were too busy to be disturbed by his behavior.

During February and March, we sorted furniture and household items to be claimed by one of the three of us, sold, or given away. For spring term and the summer, the girls rented one floor of a house in town. Erika and I met regularly and talked a lot about her classes, her friends, and, of course, money. All surface subjects. We both admitted we were emotionally exhausted and needed time to process the past, agreeing to field questions when we felt comfortable.

* *

In early May, my colleague Byron invited teacher Ginny and me to join him on his twenty-five-foot sailboat at a nearby lake. I was scared beyond words and only agreed to go if my friend promised a rescue. I never moved from my seat above a storage locker, nor did I take my hand off the lifeline behind me. My life vest was tightly fastened, and even with the cool, gentle breeze, I sweated inside its entire shape. We sailed until sunset, after which I thanked Byron and said I had used up my allotted time on the water.

But something pulled me toward the boat and sailing again. I took a few more cruises as Byron's guest, each time letting go of the lifeline a bit longer and loosening the vest a half inch. I was finally able to breathe normally. To say that I'd come to enjoy the boat and the water would be a stretch, but the challenge drew me to become more familiar with both.

Byron offered to teach me to steer and to tack. I hardly ever turn down an opportunity to learn a new skill and found myself watching the sail move smoothly across the center to the other side. I also saw it flap and flop in a small breeze and worried that in strong winds, I would lose control and fall overboard. But Byron's repeated demonstrations—and my growing trust in his competence—pushed me to finally try steering while he maneuvered the sail.

Later, I worked at handling the sail, too, and tacked in a gentle wind. I brought the mainsail across the bow and sent us forward. The several times I tried it, I found this effort satisfying, having proved to myself that I could learn the basics of sailing. I can't say I was ever relaxed in that boat, even in a light wind, but I had stayed the course and claimed new strength.

One Saturday in September, two friends joined Byron and me for a two-day trip around the thirty-five-foot-deep lake. Midafternoon, we motored toward an anchor spot near a cove. A strong wind kicked up, and the boat bounced and heeled. I buckled my life vest, and by early evening, while I helped organize dinner in the galley, with gusts still rocking the boat, I hadn't taken it off. Finally, I peered at the buckles and thought, *You have sailing skills, and Byron is highly competent.* The breeze never made it below deck, so I continued to sweat.

By the time we swallowed our first bites of the barbecued salmon, potato salad, and cucumber slices, the wind had quieted. From the bow, the dessert wine matched perfectly with the fading light and the rising moon. Slight breezes sent tiny ripples over the water. Bob, whose wife had died from cancer, slid beside me. He looked out at the lake and said softly, "I had to face life without Helen ripple by ripple."

Ripples.

The small waves it took for my children to sail a paper boat across their wading pool.

The kind of water we saw when we first stood at the Inn River, the expectation of a leisurely lunch by its side.

The repeated steps it took for me to tack and sail.

And the numerous tiny waves (and large ones, too) it would take to get to the other side of grief, guilt, and pain.

My goal: to move and tack in any wind. To become whole again for myself, for Brian, Erika, and Oskar, and for every person I love.

One day and one ripple at a time.

༄

That same September, I set up my fifth-grade classroom in another school. Since it was a Spanish immersion program, I could teach world cultures as well as United States history. A student-created reading and writing center became "The Corner to the World," with books from Native American, African, Spanish, Asian, and Scandinavian themes and cultures as examples. I wrote lessons, activities, and games with the year culminating in an event called Countries and Cultures Celebration.

My students' studies triggered a reflection that Brian never got to write about another country or culture or even his own. But I knew that our European tour allowed him to reflect on his ancestry and where many of the artists and musicians he admired came from.

Erika and I had lunch or dinner together often that year, and we always praised our forward thinking: her hard work toward a degree that would lead to a solid job, and my teaching with a new perspective.

The divorce had been finalized, and the country property had closed. I was reassured by the choices my daughter was making. At the house she now shared with two friends, I saw how much the friendships meant to her. We always found a moment for sharing lighter experiences, like how Swift Arrow kept other cats and big dogs at bay with simple blinks.

When the school year ended, Byron and I started dating. Because he had never known Brian, his insights about my son allowed fresh dialogue and input. He invited me to sail the Pacific Northwest on his new forty-foot boat. In midsummer, we took sailing lessons in the waters off the Dorset and East Devon coastal areas of southern England. My world widened. And, although I noticed I was happier more often, it was a surface happiness. I had worked to keep thoughts of the tragedy and divorce from taking hold again, but I left figuring out how to process them for later.

One pleasant weekend after returning from England, Byron and I set sail from Newport, Oregon, up the coast. The winds stayed calm for two hours, and I decided I could manage both the sails and the wheel for a bit. I made a few perfect tacks and turns until the wind changed direction and came back with forceful waves that sent the mainsail pitching almost parallel with the water. Determined not to look incompetent, I tacked and swung the wheel at random until Byron came to my rescue.

The boat in experienced hands, I knelt mid-deck and raised my arms. Water had multiple levels and surprises, and the art of sailing had levels I had not yet mastered, especially when outside the confines of a lake. I closed my eyes and absorbed the thought that God had multiple levels for everything. I had only taken advantage of a few.

I needed to connect every step of this new life to the Higher Power so I could settle the tragedy into its rightful place. His insights, partnered with my own creative solutions, would move me forward.

I kept myself busy with my job, writing a book for teachers, managing my mother's rental properties in Seattle, and sailing. Steering through headwinds on Byron's boat taught me I could navigate other kinds of headwinds and waters. I prayed that the tools to face old and new issues head-on would present themselves, and I would recognize God's presence in each.

By the spring of 1990, I had finished my book with lessons and activities from world cultures. Erika had her first professional job, her degree almost in hand; Oskar's company had transferred him to San Francisco; and I had finally sold all my mother's rentals. The world called to me. It felt right to look outward across continents and oceans. Long ago, from the window of my father's two-door Ford, I had dreamed of visiting European castles where people wore costumes. Mom always said that when I believed something felt right, it was best to get to it.

I had developed an alternative mindset during the time I learned to sail and taught the countries and cultures unit. Yearning for a first-hand understanding of how other people lived, what they believed, and their specific insights regarding the natural world's gifts to life,

I sought enlightenment that would bring Brian's loving spirit close again. While my family's European trip had focused on enjoying the sights and sounds of a country, I felt that envisioning the manner in which different societies handle personal challenges would help me manage my own future with more clarity.

Byron wanted to teach overseas, too, so we went to a job fair—as friends once again. I had decided that my first priority was to explore who I was at the moment, who I strived to be, and how I would contribute to the world. I felt a relationship would not allow me the mindset to realize those goals. Byron had been a colleague since my first year back to teaching, and as a longtime friend, he agreed to respect my wishes to move forward without the more intense emotional obligations.

An international school in Colombia hired us both for the next school year, me as the librarian and him as a middle school teacher. Swift Arrow, now my cat, and I would share living quarters.

I could not have foreseen how this opportunity would reset my life.

TWENTY-ONE
PEOPLE, PLACES, AND RESET

The week after I arrived at the school, east of Barranquilla, a local faculty couple invited me to a dinner of *bandeja paisa*, the Colombian national dish. Candles, lanterns, and colored lights decorated the cool outdoor area where, at about nine o'clock, a table with platters of grilled steak, sausage, white rice, and beans topped with fried egg and avocado greeted guests. I had eaten each of the foods separately many times, but this combination, infused with cumin, cilantro, and unfamiliar salsa spices, sent my taste buds on a fascinating journey.

After we sampled desserts of *cocadas blancas*—shredded coconut "cookies"—*coconut flan*, and *arroz con leche*, the couple's two children presented us with handmade gifts. I received a jellyfish made with a paper baking cup and tissue paper streamers, and a paper-plate monkey-face mask. I hugged both children, tied on the mask, and ran with them while waving the jellyfish. We finally collapsed on the grass with giggles and high fives.

These evening gatherings, including the art creations, became something of a regular event. As their friend, I helped the children make gifts for guests. Grinning while trimming a monkey's yarn tail three times, I felt like a member of this inside crowd.

The school's mostly local student body in grades kindergarten through high school came to my library for lessons and book checkouts; their friendliness and regular reading of recommended books impressed me. Engaging with the children left little time for sadness or loneliness.

When the air conditioning failed, Byron and I, along with local teachers, traveled to the turquoise Pacific Ocean and the rugged area of Tayrona Park. We stayed in a wood-framed bungalow and hiked to the beach through a jungle alive with three kinds of monkeys, some of the rarest birds on earth, and insects that remained nameless. We took long breaths below giant rocks to absorb the natural energy and observe how the creatures cared for themselves and each other. I found joy in watching plants and animals thrive, and my skin, bones, mind, and heart soaked up water's soothing properties.

My hometown friend listened to me describe incidents from Brian's childhood where he had rescued birds or helped classmates learn their times tables. The robin's-egg-blue waters inspired me to cast these memories over the ocean and to chuckle, if only for a moment. Byron listened intently, hardly ever offering advice.

Peter, a contact in Cartagena, invited me on a tour of the historic yellow colonial buildings, draped with magenta, orange, and purple bougainvillea. My gracious host spent two days leading walks along quiet streets in front of the stately homes and churches, the famous flowers streaming from windows and balconies. Beauty filled me with appreciation.

Peter's family treated me like an old friend. He and his mother, both attorneys, worked for modest salaries and had organized a nonprofit that funded art education. Inspired by their selfless spirit, I bought a framed oil of a simple colonial home resembling theirs, painted by a teacher in the program. It included buttercup yellow and purple bougainvillea. I contributed to their public-school art teacher endowment and still draw energy and enjoyment today from partnering with locals to recognize the value of imagination.

In January, I joined fellow teacher Vera for a weekend to explore nearby lush tropical coffee plantations. We set out to find Val and Nic, a couple who had recently taken over the family's small coffee business. With their two preschool-aged children snuggled close, we drank tasty brew on the front porch and learned how they made a modest living with the limited acreage. "The volcanic soil, annual rainfall, and high altitude give us a bountiful harvest," Nic said. The family's genuine happiness stirred me to stand up and clap.

I couldn't wait for February and Barranquilla's Carnival with its signature grand parade, the Battle of the Flowers. On Saturday, the first day of the festival, "The Arrow" and I arrived in the early morning, the cat perched atop my shoulder. Floats and groups playing traditional Colombian instruments passed along the crowded street, accompanying ethnic dancers in colorful, flowery costumes.

In the middle of the six-hour parade, a *cumbia* group gathered a block away, and I went to stand nearby. I wanted to learn the steps of this national dance and had fashioned a costume for the slower, more laid-back ancestor of salsa. The red-and-blue skirt, white peasant blouse, and large red hair bow with a small orchid seemed right. Swift Arrow's harness sported an identical ribbon. The partners practiced their routines on a side street, and when I heard a dancer say, "*Rapida, rapida, lenta*"—quick, quick, slow—I copied the step as best I could.

I stayed beside the group and their band when they joined the parade with flutes and drums playing "La Pollera Colora." Later, we merrymakers stepped in time to the music, sweeping our arms upward and twirling toward a partner or alone. As a child, when I danced with my father, I struggled with my two left feet, but then and now, I let myself enjoy the fun.

Occasionally, my lower back hurt, but with breaks, I reveled in delight . . . until sunup.

Immersion with the Colombian people, their lives, and livelihoods, togetherness with the country's wild and serene natural areas, and delight in the flower festival's dances set me on a path I was eager to continue. The authentic voices, tastings, and unselfish caring brought new insights about my own family, culture, and country. I began to understand who I had been and was now—with the strong desire to learn who I was determined to become.

I was ready for more life-altering moments. While still in Colombia, I accepted a two-year kindergarten position at an international school in Damascus. After a brief visit home, Swift Arrow and I again said goodbye to family and friends. The hallmark values of the archaeological riches of Syria passed down through the ages, including the Great Mosque in Damascus, the ruins of Palmyra, and the Citadel in Aleppo, beckoned me.

The day after I settled into my apartment in a residential area of Damascus, I took a cab to the Al-Hamidiyah Souq, with its two-thousand-foot-long space in the old walled city. Near its entrance stand the six columns of the temple to the Roman god Jupiter and the courtyard of the Great Mosque. It was a beautiful afternoon, and I reflected on the mosque's history, warmed by the thought that both Christians and Muslims had worshipped on the same soil. A Christian church once stood there.

I walked through the souq's many covered streets and spotted hand-carved furniture, intricately designed and hammered copper plates, and all manner of spices and sweets. A recent urge to learn belly dancing sent me perusing the diverse collection of outfits. I bought a black ensemble with gold and silver trimmings and was told I could take lessons from a dancer trained in traditional technique.

Alone in my apartment after having admired bodies that bent, twisted, and stretched perfectly, I checked out how my own torso, arms, and hips would move in the costume. I was impressed with the information that the art and architecture of Palmyra, Syria's show-case ancient city, had accommodated multiple societies and cultures. Anxious to bring that energy into my body and expand my limited range of motion, a few days later, I stood in the amphitheater's ruins wearing my new outfit. I practiced isolating my hips while moving my chest and arms and imagined dancers long ago entertaining others in this fashion. I'll never forget the connection and passion of that day. I couldn't wait to learn the right technique.

A teacher and three friends assembled at my apartment for les-sons. At each session, light from fragrant candles and Arabic folk-loric rhythms nudged us to isolate our heads, ribcages, and abdo-mens, linking bones and muscles for movement to sway back and forth. Strings of tiny gold beads and coins on the three-piece outfit kept time. My bodily structures were learning to engage with each other, and my mind and heart reached back to the art of Roman, Greek, and Persian pillars and columns that connected past cultures, peoples, and values. I found strength in those pillars.

The following fall, I joined a family of Syrian women for a wake. We had become friends, and two days after the funeral of an aunt, the grieving group gathered at the home of the deceased. The Syrian women were dressed in typical public clothing—a long navy raincoat or *khimar* and a white headscarf—while I, as a Westerner, wore a black blouse and skirt. A sister of the deceased read from the Koran, and daughters and nieces recited prayers. Proper respect and decorum called for the women to avoid eye contact. The rite reminded me somewhat of a simple Christian memorial service.

Later, when we sipped tea, the ladies looked softly into each other's eyes. The message was clear: *We are sisters.* Thoughts arose of my family's lack of closure from never finding Brian, but I felt a reassurance that life must go on in spite of loss. This promised deeper levels of letting go of pain. I vowed to maintain a can-do attitude, practice patience to keep digging, and allow myself to consider issues of guilt that had held me back.

My teaching assistant, Jamela, had lived through years of difficult political times with her Syrian father and Czech mother. We talked for hours about savoring today for today. She told me that each morning, whether she woke to sun, rain, or snow, she said, "I am alive and strong."

Often, during those two years, I danced in all kinds of weather, with snow falling for the first time in years. I kept repeating, "Faith has brought you this far, and the ongoing journey promises more blessings than you can count." After all, my daughter was thriving in her chosen profession and I had made wonderful new international friends, taught children from all over the world who loved to learn, and been able to step outside myself to look at who I had become.

I often kiss the photos I took of Syria and its people, including my classes of kindergarteners. I send energy for their wisdom wherever they are. I kept in touch with my friend for several years but eventually lost contact.

The archaeological treasures, although many have since been damaged or destroyed, still live in my heart. The Krak des Chevaliers—the Crusaders' castle two hours' drive from Damascus, once considered by T. E. Lawrence to be the best preserved and most admirable castle anywhere—was damaged but still stands. I understand it currently welcomes visitors. During my visit, the solid exterior lime walls, the cavernous Hall of the Knights—a stunning example of Crusader architecture—and the red and blue-green frescos in the chapel spoke strength to me.

Author's Note: I was fortunate to live in Syria long before the present Assad regime and before the earthquake of February 2023. I pray for the Syrian people constantly. The news stories about destroyed schools and classrooms make the present devastation so vivid. I continue to donate to humanitarian organizations, including those that care for starving cats and other animals. I have to believe that my teaching assistant, Jamela, is no longer in Damascus.

Byron stayed in Colombia until the end of the next school year, paid off his boat, and began a world cruise. I met him in Kusadasi, Turkey, after my Syria stint, and we sailed to several Greek islands. We were impressed with how the islanders provided for one another physically, financially, and spiritually. No one suffered without the community sharing their pain and pitching in to help.

After two years back in the US, my desire to go further afield socially and culturally found me contracted to teach a six-year-old prince for the royal family of Saudi Arabia. I couldn't pass up the opportunity to tutor a child with his lineage and to learn about this exotic country of contrasts.

Karim's big brown eyes, tentative smile, and wavy hair endeared him to me immediately. After reading Marcia Brown's picture book

Stone Soup, he wrinkled his nose when, presumably for the first time, he sliced cabbage, carrots, and onions. He dropped them into a kettle with the designated stone and said, "This soup is for the king in the story, and for me and my friends."

We invented fun projects all year and even planned a trip into the nearby desert called the Great Nufad to study sand cats. Supposedly, a small number lived in burrows there.

Karim's longing to see a sand cat, one of the smallest wild cats in the world, prompted me to join the Riyadh chapter of the Hash House Harriers, an international running and social group, to scope out presumed habitats. Friday drives outside the city to jog in shorts, having shed the normal women's black abaya and head covering, also gave me a chance to weave around saltbushes and across the sand for exercise and to search for various desert creatures.

I camped several Friday nights in a sleeping bag, in hopes of catching sight of one or more of the cats. I recalled how Brian and I had knelt for hours to watch ladybugs feast on aphids, and how Erika and I often spread our sleeping bags to watch shooting stars. I did *glimpse* one cat—they are true loners—and although Karim was never able to camp in the desert, our research enabled him to write a story. He described the cat's dense fur and extra-large ears, how it crawled out of its burrow during the cool night and padded across the desert to hunt. The young prince drew a picture of the cat's thick fur pads that lifted its feet off the sand. He titled the story "The No-Tracks Cat" and told me he would keep this work forever.

Karim and his family would move to the UK when his older siblings were ready for college. I have faith that the vision he caught through writing and illustrating books about animals, his family, his culture, and reading picture books like *Arrow to the Sun*, *Mufaro's Beautiful Daughters*, and *People* would inform his values as an adult.

And I'm grateful to my children's literature professor, who started me on the path to reading widely, and who constantly reminded me after Erika graduated how much I would love overseas teaching.

The dynamics and contrasts around gender, religion, and politics fascinated me. Much of the time while in the Kingdom, I felt like an observer of the culture, which allowed me a measure of objectivity. I asked questions and worked to respect the different points of view of my responders.

When I was out in public in a bank, a store, or a restaurant, I had to obey gender-specific customs, rules, and restrictions. In the walled and guarded compound where I lived, I was free to dress, eat, and behave as I did in the West. And, in the desert, our whereabouts were kept secret so no Saudi men could show up to watch. Only once did I note cars of them lined up to see women running in shorts and tank tops.

My Saudi female friends had encouraged me to learn what the real culture had to offer, apart from the restrictive norms. Although they embraced mothering and nurturing, they wanted to be an integral part of the business and academic world. One of them staged a drive-through of Riyadh in 1992 to demonstrate that a female could take care of her family in an emergency. In the early 2000s, she visited me in the US. To this day, I admire her belief in change.

Longer weekend trips to the distant desert with the Harriers freed me to explore more landscapes and to spend quality time with expats from around the world. Because of restrictions the political system claimed were stipulated by the Koran, no Saudi men or women were allowed to be part of this international group. For Christmas, we draped red-and-green paper chains and silver tinsel across the branches of a tamarisk tree, laid down a parquet floor, and sank candles in the sand nearby.

After toasts and a dinner smorgasbord of delicacies from thirty countries, the music started. The Beatles' "I'm Happy Just to Dance with You" played on a boombox while people rock-stepped and swung their arms on the large rectangular floor. "Joy to the World" brought another group of swing dancers, including Santa and Mrs. Claus—in red shirts, shorts, and hats. I twirled, sometimes with a partner and sometimes by myself, basking in the warmth of the evening and the camaraderie of Japanese, German, and Chilean businesspeople. I thought about the lovely Saudi women who weren't even allowed to watch us run or dance. They dreamed of one day swaying and swinging, with or without an abaya.

The after-dinner Christmas Eve party continued with a rumba to "White Christmas." When the dance floor grew crowded, I moved onto the sand, stretched my feet beyond our camp, and reached across silver and blue shadows toward the full moon. The music drifted upward, and the stars sparkled like a thousand mirror balls.

Cumbia dancing in Colombia, belly dancing in Syria, and ballroom steps in the Saudi desert changed me forever. Every satisfying and heartwarming experience from these years allowed me to reach into my pocket of grief and dissolve another piece of the pain.

My generation was not known for its ability to find and express deep feelings. Oskar was not the only one who had difficulty figuring out what he felt and finding the courage to share it. Women have traditionally been expected to "grin and bear it," an attitude I took literally from my mother. This meant some pieces of advice I gave Erika were, in retrospect, not helpful.

After losing Brian, we each had our own failures as parents to our remaining child. However, the blunders humbled me and taught me to think before I speak.

The physical and emotional distance gave me fresh understanding of who I was destined to become, and I had learned it wasn't so scary to open my mind, body, and heart to both triumphs and missteps. Each had teachable moments. I had successfully paddled through moderate ripples to learn from other peoples and places and was ready for larger and deeper meaning. Finding the courage to reach beyond perceived limitations, I couldn't wait to learn how to better process and communicate the specifics of grief and its feelings.

The four of us and then the three of us enjoyed large and small adventures and everyday life. I had loved being Erika's mother through the thick and thin of childhood and believe I gave her the best of myself. I also cherish having been Oskar's wife until there was nothing left to give.

An abundance of new knowledge awaited me.

TWENTY-TWO
EXERCISE, CONNECTIONS, AND A VOICE

I came back to the US for another school year in Oregon. Two days after I welcomed students, I loaded my car with a white silk bridal gown, bridesmaids' ensembles, and a mother-of-the-bride blue silk dress. Erika would marry Tim on September 8 at Roche Harbor Resort in the San Juan Islands, having dated and fallen in love with him after college. His family had lived in our country home neighborhood.

When my daughter was ten, the three of us had camped on this same island and ridden our bikes to the picturesque hillside community church overlooking the bay. Erika had gazed thoughtfully at the quaint structure and said, "Someday, I will get married here."

Today was that day. The sun welcomed us, filtering through the pines and firs as she made her way up the steps on the arm of her father. She took measured paces down the aisle, her face softly expressing, *I've pictured this day for a long time.* Oskar kept his head, shoulders, and arms straight, showing his intention to get this right. I saw twinkles of expression pass between them.

Our friend pastor Dan shared bits of wisdom the couple still cherish today. The buffet in the Hotel De Haro dining room featured elegant home cooking, and Erika and I savored an appetizer of toasted goat cheese crostini, cedar-plank-grilled salmon, and savory green beans. I took small helpings, knowing I needed to be available for questions and to welcome our guests.

It was a stretch to believe Oskar had dealt with his alcoholism, but he appeared stable most of the time and danced with his daughter and with me. When the couple prepared to leave, I said, "I see staying power with you two, no matter what." My heart was more peaceful about Erika than at any time since losing her brother.

I wrapped up my teaching career in 2000 and spent two years writing additional language arts and social studies handbooks for teachers. A strong pull to restart regular exercise took me on treks and hikes through forested trails. The bountiful upward climbs had multiple rewards, and I decided they would be my primary workout.

I loved the forty-seven-hundred-acre natural wilderness area with its one-thousand-foot peak and bark-mulch and gravel paths, only a short drive away. A typical hike took me through a white oak savanna where a lizard often darted across my shoes; a pinkish-cinnamon coyote, sure of the direction he wanted to take, would trot into the distance; and sometimes a peregrine falcon swooped down to the nearby grasses for a lunchtime feed. The hikes prompted me to notice the aerodynamics of an eagle and the uniqueness of each spore on the back of a sword fern. I ran through grasses and could almost feel the pulse of each vein when my finger moved up and down a blade of soft green. I ignored the scratches from drier grasses.

I cooled off in the woods beside Oregon grape branches with shiny, slender leaves and yellow flowers. A final push to the top of the rise allowed me to sit on a rock and take in views of the valley and its river. When binoculars brought the more distant western

Coast Range and Eastern Cascades into focus, they showed a myriad of red-orange, yellow, and magenta hues in the sky. The air gently moved, filling me with a grapefruit-like scent from crushed Doug fir needles, and my heart rate slowed. I felt the cleansing breaths deep inside my lungs.

On a late spring afternoon, the upward trail of a park replete with paths brought me to a saucer magnolia tree covered with reddish-purple and white blossoms. A few days later, the blossoms covered the grass and soil, petals facing front or back, curled up, and pointing in all directions. The interesting configuration invited me to crawl around and examine dozens, smiling at their distinctiveness.

Exercise had become much more than staying in shape physically. The falcon's ardor and the grasses' straight-up pose were powerful forces from the living God. They served as models of strength to me.

In August of 2009, after a tour of Turkey's ancient sites, I traveled to the Greek island of Patmos, where the disciple John is said to have written the biblical Book of Revelation. I climbed the hill from the harbor to the holy cave where he received his visions. Inside, the air was refreshing, candles glowed, and I prayed for inspiration to focus my mind and heart. Steady chants opened me to a spiritual force that let me unpack issues of grief that still weighed me down.

Later, on that same trip, soaking in the waters of the Dead Sea, an energy coursed through my legs, torso, and arms, gently releasing more pain and guiding me to look at my part in Brian's drowning. I had never held myself responsible for his death the way Oskar seemed to, but the nagging thought that I had endorsed the decision to go to the river that day was still with me.

My soul had to believe once and for all that hindsight is twenty-twenty, and I had called it with the most accurate input I had that day . . .

I folded my hands in thanksgiving for the insight while moisture spread over my face, chest, and limbs, and my body relaxed from cheeks to neck to toes. It felt healing to be in this state.

The other burning issue was my present relationship with Brian. My heart felt the connection with him and his life gradually grow dimmer and dimmer. I longed for a tangible energy when I picked up his recorder or kissed his picture.

The message resonated from the chants: *Be patient* . . .

In June of 2011, I signed up for a ballroom rumba class with a woman named Laura. Lower back pain had become more frequent, and unhealthy practices such as bending over student desks for years, long-term crises and grieving, and lack of regular exercise during the busiest times had significantly compressed two of my lumbar disks. Surgery was recommended. After recovery, my doctor advised me to add exercise to walking and weights that would augment my core strength. Dance had been on my mind since the nights of swaying and turning with my father and the brief encounters in Colombia, Syria, and Saudi Arabia. I saw the value of specific steps, routines, and positions to strengthen my core.

I hurried into a dome-shaped gymnasium where several couples moved to the sound of "The Way You Look Tonight," the leads and follows seeming to stride in perfect harmony while I watched. This partner dance looked complicated, and I was sure I had come upon an advanced class.

I headed outside and down the stairs. A voice from behind me said, "Are you Janice? I'm Laura." I turned and looked into the face of a small, short-haired woman whose savvy appearance spoke trust. Slowly walking toward her, I nodded and said, "Is this really a beginner class?"

She touched my shoulder, assuring me it was and that I would be welcomed into the group. Back inside, Laura introduced me to a student named Paula. I sat down and, as I took off my street shoes, asked her if this was her first rumba class. "Oh, no, it's my third. Put your dance shoes on and get ready to have fun," she said. I stared at my worn sandals lying upside down on the floor, flipped them over with one foot, and slid into them.

Fifty people formed a line and stepped in a *slow, quick, quick* walk around the room. I joined them and told myself that if this was rumba, I could do it. Next, Laura gave instructions for the basic box step for leads and for follows. Each lead and each follow practiced separately and then met a partner. Mine was named Joe.

I did move back with my right foot and to the side with my left, but I blanked on what to do next. When I moved forward, I stepped on Joe. After landing on his foot twice, I squeezed his hand so hard he stiffened. My eyes watered, and I blinked at my sandals. During the rest of the hour, it was difficult to avoid crunching my partner's toes, and I wondered why I found this so difficult when it looked easy.

Laura complimented everyone for a great lesson, but I left questioning whether I would learn to follow another person. At home, I spoke the backward, forward, and side steps out loud and danced them with music. I thought if I committed them to muscle memory, I could focus on being led.

I saw little progress and stumbled through the series. My ego had taken a hit, and I was certain I was a dunce as a dancer. Maybe dance wasn't the right choice for an added exercise. Stress over my difficulty learning these movements might outweigh any benefits from conditioning my body.

Free-form dance I could do, and I went to outdoor venues where bands played during the summer. I couldn't keep my feet still.

In the fall, something told me to keep taking classes, and I signed up for Laura's foxtrot lessons. I learned the steps more readily, but here, too, I often misread where or when the lead directed me to go.

In early January, I stood up from bed and acknowledged that the numbness in my left leg had increased. I committed to workouts, walks, or yoga every day, and to taking one more series of dance lessons. Laura's cross-step waltz class started in a week.

She introduced the basics, with everyone counting *one, two, three* and stepping in the simplest pattern. At the end of my first dance with Joe, he said, "I heard you saying numbers while you followed me." His compliment motivated me to count every step. For the first time, I had a bit of hope that I would learn to dance. At least for now, counting occupied my mind so my body could respond to the lead's shoulders and core. Laura and the other dancers noticed my improvement.

I had come to understand that free-form dancing at summer festivals and being led by a partner could both have a place in my life. Waltz and foxtrot are easier because they are danced *on* the beat, while rumba is danced *against* it.

True partner dancing remained elusive because I only sporadically relaxed enough to feel the connection. Long-term leadership roles in both my professional and personal life had taught me to "take charge" every time I saw a situation that needed leadership. I finally had to acknowledge there are occasions when, even if I know how to lead, following is the right choice.

I conditioned my core, practiced the steps, and danced them

every day. And I climbed hills and lifted weights. The numbness in my leg stabilized while I counted through additional rumba and cross-step waltz classes. Fresh energy and actual enjoyment propelled me to continue, and I began to reap cardiovascular benefits and improved muscle control. My core felt stronger.

In December, after the final class, I attended a local ballroom club's holiday dance, believing I was ready to follow routines and patterns with any lead. During the cross-step waltz song "Blackberry Winter," I stepped on a new partner's toes multiple times. "So sorry," I said, grabbing my coat, purse, and street shoes and fleeing down the stairs.

Rain poured as I slogged through puddles, water squishing between my toes. I pushed on the gas pedal and headed home. In my driveway, I unstrapped the shoes and kicked them into nearby bushes. Ballroom dance was supposed to be a prime enjoyment for my life going forward. That didn't appear to be happening.

A week later, I said to myself, *You're not a quitter. You've always gotten back to the rhythm and stepped in the pattern.* I pulled the stiff two-inchers out of the dirt and set them on a shelf in the garage. Repeatedly, I heard these words from their muddy surface: *Let your body read* every *detail of the connection with your partner.*

At Laura's suggestion, I signed up for an Argentine tango class known to promote partner connection. The following week, instructor Maria demonstrated how, if I lifted my core to bring strength through my back, I would feel the lead's weight on his foot, and focus on reading his core and shoulders.

I took the lessons, practiced the strategy hundreds of times, and when my partner came toward me at the last class, I breathed, centering my body toward his. With his hands on my forearms, he moved forward with his left foot. I stepped back with my right and waited for the next step, and the next. We continued around the floor in close embrace. I felt led through every muscle. My partner grinned.

There would always be times when I wouldn't know which foot was the right one, but I would dance on. And now, stepping and whirling felt like magic.

In late February, dressed in a black sheath dress, white pillbox hat, and dark bobbed wig, I drove to a celebrities-themed ballroom dance. I ran up the stairs and twirled through the open door where gold and silver streamers swayed under the mirror ball. The spinning facets sparkled.

An Oscar trophy and photos of movie stars decorated the table where I sat. Joe gave me a thumbs-up, and I waved to other friends. As the lights dimmed and the foxtrot tune "A Wink and a Smile" began to play, I slipped on my shimmering dance sandals. A ballroom classmate held out his hand, we faced each other, and I slid my right foot back. My partner led the zigzag step at the corners, and I stayed with him.

When the dance finished, he said, "You've been practicing."

I smiled.

"Moon River" began, and a dancer who introduced himself as Jack led me through the *one, two, three* counts of a waltz. "Let's dance again," he said.

During intermission, the announcer said, "Jackie O, come and claim first prize for the celebrity costume contest." A minor affirmation, but combined with the others, it was evidence of the shift I was making toward connecting my body and soul.

I gathered my purse and shoe bag to go home, but something said, "Stay for the last dance." I took a breath and sat down.

The glow in the ballroom softened, and a guitarist began strumming "Stand by Me" while tiny reflections from the mirror ball swirled across the floor, walls, and ceiling. They reminded me of Brian fingering the tiny holes on his recorder while I sang the lyrics to this song. My tears fell onto the white paper tablecloth, and Joe covered the wet with piles of napkins. He held my hand, drew me close, and said, "Let's dance this beautiful rumba."

His arm around my back, we walked to a spot in the center of the floor. I closed my eyes and took a step backward. The words *don't be afraid* infused every cell of me with hope. I glided as if I had been dancing all my life.

The song ended, and we stood in silence.

Then through the quiet, a voice came.

Mom.

I clutched Joe and gazed upward.

Come back to Austria. I'll be waiting.

Brian.

I floated down the stairs and into the night.

In my driveway, I looked up to the gleaming sky and lifted my arms.

"I'm coming!"

TWENTY-THREE
THE JOURNEY TO BRIAN

The next morning, I booked a flight to Innsbruck for June 4. Days later, I questioned my initial excitement and wondered what Brian's words, *I'll be waiting*, meant. He had been lost to the river beyond our ability to save him or even to find his body.

He said he'd be waiting in Austria. I trusted that meant *somewhere* in the area around Innsbruck where we had visited. For most of my life, I had believed in surprise, mystery, and miracles. Either Brian would send me a sign where he was, or I would find a sign myself. I didn't know if he would appear as the nine-year-old I had carried in my heart, with eyes that danced and lips that reached toward pink cheeks, or the fifty-year-old of 2012? What would make him *real* to me?

A few weeks later, I met a friend for lunch and shared my concerns. She said, "You have always listened to your inner voice, and good things have happened." I sat still for a moment, hugged her, and said I would keep listening. And trusting. I had told family and friends only that I had scheduled a stopover in Austria on my way to Jordan, and thankfully, no one questioned my solo mission.

Over the next few months, I imagined I would find Brian whispering, "Daisies tell of love" as he ran through fields of them, or fingering his recorder at a town music festival, or maybe giving food to hungry cats. I saw myself running toward him, saying, "This moment will stay forever!" I pushed away the possibility that the voice above the mirror ball was a trick of the mind, while the image of finding Brian on the Inn River was too horrific to think about. I still carried echoes of his harsh journey downstream and afterward.

I would trust.

As the plane entered Austria, I watched the jade-green Inn River through my window. From a distance, it carved a tranquil path along the base of low mountains and white-capped Tyrolean Alps, guiding us toward its namesake, Innsbruck. As we came nearer to the strip of water, its flow became ominous, and I gripped the armrests, taking fast, shallow breaths. The young woman next to me touched my hand and asked if I was okay. Eyes closed, I nodded. After several tension-filled minutes, the plane bounced down the runway and stopped.

"May I help you with your backpack?" a flight attendant said. I opened my eyes to the only bin with luggage—mine. In the terminal, the thought that I was closer than ever to my son kept me moving. I sipped water and found the rental car office. That evening, I would drive to a hotel in Old Town, and the next morning, I'd call at the power company office before heading to Landeck, the town closest to the accident site.

A narrow road took me through neighborhoods where I couldn't hear the river. I pretended it didn't exist and rolled down my windows. Then, as I came near town, the roaring made me jerk my head to the right. There it was: hundreds of feet across and gray-white with rapids, barren terrain along its banks. The churning expanse cast a sinister reflection on the day Brian drowned. I was overwhelmed with the impulse to get far away.

In 1972, we had seen the Inn River from a road a bit south of Innsbruck, where the flow had been half this width and speed. The white-and-green hues of the waves had been beautiful and soothing. Driving west and upriver, we had seen through binoculars vegetation that shielded the water and fish, as well as the flowers and trees that thrived on the hillside leading to the stream. Because of the increased need for power and more dams, I suspected the river near Nesselgarten and the drowning site also looked different today. How, I didn't know.

Would I need to face or think about this water every day during the visit? My foot slipped off the clutch, and the car lurched, stopping just short of the bumper ahead. I pulled onto a side road on the right, rolled up the windows, and took long, deep breaths while I studied the map. The only access to my hotel was over the river across a bridge. One of them was in front of me.

In the line of traffic, I forced my eyes to stay open and on the road while recognizing the water's own journey. In the middle of the bridge, I glanced at the ominous flow under me and sped to the hotel. Parking by the door, I put my hands over my ears against the thunderous roar across the street and repeated, *I am here to meet my son.*

"It's so close," I said out loud.

The hotel doorman tapped the glass and pointed to the parking lot along the water's fencing. I raised my hand in an "okay," sighed, backed up, and parked in the first vacant space. Inside the hotel, I hoped I had remembered to put on the emergency brake.

My fear of water and the Inn's claim of my son settled anew inside me. Napping in my room, I drifted off, dreaming I was fighting my way back and forth across the river, holding onto a rope. As I inched my body through the frigid current that tried to pull me downstream, I told myself, *I am strong; I can do this.* Although I woke up crying, "I can't!" I reaffirmed why I was here and promised myself I would get to Brian.

Pushing through the revolving door, I stepped across the street toward the roiling flow. My son's message, *I'll be waiting,* gave me the courage I needed. For the next few days, like it or not, the Inn would be part of my life. At the top of the bank, I peered at the silt-laden water and shouted, "Let me be and I'll do the same!" I turned away, unable to avoid thinking of the sleepy eel my family had seen as we began our seemingly harmless exploration of the riverbank.

While I ate breakfast the next morning, I located the library on a map, as I needed to check if additional news articles had been posted. The one we had read described the drowning and cited the utility's negligence in releasing water without proper warning. Apparently, only the one article had been written. I had hoped that additional voices were documented, which would accord me a stronger case with the power company to help enforce safety measures for the gamut of river enthusiasts. From what I had read, some measures had been enacted and signs erected, but not enough of either.

At the utility offices, I was eventually put in touch with a spokesperson who took me to visit nearby dams. It was enlightening to know there had been a degree of improvement in the containment of flow, duration, and speed, and posting of signs for visitors, but the relief I sought eluded me. I couldn't confirm comprehensive signage or significant monitoring for public and visitor safety. Water is big business, and most of the advancements I saw were the result of the requirements of commerce, not concern for ordinary citizens.

It was late afternoon when I sank into my car's seat. I sipped tea and headed west and slightly south on the autobahn, the river paralleling the road and becoming somewhat narrower and greener the farther upstream I drove. In the midevening light, shadows hovered over the Alps. I found a radio station playing Mozart's Serenade Number 13 in G, the piece evoking memories of Brian playing the composer's work. The water looked iridescent. I hardly noticed the vehicles that rushed to pass my small car.

It was dusk when a sign reading LANDECK came into focus. I made a left turn and, several minutes later, drove to the entrance of the saffron-colored Hotel Schrofenstein. This lodging was in a different area from where we had stayed before, and I took note of the Inn flowing behind the building as I parked, almost wishing I had tried to book our former hotel.

When I passed my reservation to a woman wearing a white peasant blouse and blue skirt, she held out her hand. "I'm so happy to meet you, Ms. Jensen. I am Frau Volk."

I smiled, "I'm glad to be here. It's been a long journey." Herr Volk appeared and carried my luggage to the second floor. I followed, anxious to know if I would hear the river. I had resolved that I would face it when I had to, but I could not endure its foreboding sounds while I slept. The Herr swung open the door to number fifteen, an ornately decorated room with three large windows and semi-sheer coverings. All was quiet. When he left, I sat on the bed and thought, *I can do this.*

Over a dinner of *spinatknodel* in the wood-framed blue-and-gold dining room, I considered my next step. No message had come from Brian since the mirror ball, and I thought I might sense his presence on a hillside above the river's view and sounds.

An idea made me grab a notepad and pencil. I would write messages to my son to tuck into nooks and crannies around town. In one respect, this gesture seemed far-fetched. But I didn't consider it any more equivocal than the voice under the mirror ball that had brought me back to Austria.

The four different notes said:

I'm here, my love, at the Schrofenstein Hotel.

If you don't find me first, I'll find you!

Every day since the mirror ball, I've dreamed of being with you.

I have faith we'll find each other.

I copied each three times, gathered my jacket and flashlight, and left to put them in strategic places. Two blocks up the street, I stood in the middle of a flight of stairs with a low rock wall on either side. I listened, and hearing only voices and cars in the distance, I tucked two rolled notes into spaces between the rocks. At the top, I walked along a narrow street with several Bavarian-style homes adorned with hanging flower baskets. The setting reminded me of Fliess and the goodness of Frau and Alois.

I stopped and took a breath. A soft body rubbed at my left leg, faintly squeaking, and I gasped, dropping the bag of notes. My flashlight revealed a yellow, tiger-striped cat. I bent to see eyes glowing green and hear trills pulsing through thick fur. Reaching out my hand, I blinked a bemused smile. *I'll call you Sunny.*

The cat sniffed my fingers while I rocked back to sit on the gravel. He held up a paw, and his purrs got louder and faster as I folded him close, his warm body in my arms feeling like Brian's cat. He wrapped his front legs around my neck, and I buried my face in his soft fur.

After long moments, I set him down and said, "Let's find more rocks, trees, and lampposts to hide the notes."

The cat walked ahead and sniffed at tree trunks, bushes, and rocks, twitching his whiskers when I edged a paper into a contoured nook or cranny. It was midnight when I finally snuggled Sunny one more time and said I would see him soon. He followed me.

I walked back toward the hotel and stopped at the steps to check on the notes. They were still there. Behind me, the cat licked a paw and meowed. I took his message to mean this was one moment in a process.

My hotel room felt pleasant in the low light. I lit a candle, got ready for bed, and glanced at the closed windows. I would let the quietness stay. Under the light comforter, I stretched out on my back, and thoughts flowed without direction or judgment.

I must tell Brian why I couldn't rush into the rising water to save him.

The dawn brought both a sense of familiarity and newness. Brian *had* summoned me, and I was struck by the idea that I would find him somewhere pristine because he loved order and harmony. I also suspected laughter would echo.

After a traditional Austrian breakfast of muesli, breads, cheese, cold cuts, and tomatoes, and a second cup of coffee, I motored the three miles to Nesselgarten, the Inn River downhill on my right. I turned slightly toward it several times and reaffirmed that it would not keep me from my mission. The car repair shop came into view, and I drove on, not getting a sense that Brian would be on that hill behind it. I would visit Alois later.

It seemed fitting to turn left, drive the hillside road toward Fliess, and hang out on a knoll. At the farm stay two days before the accident, Brian had sat among a field of daisies and held a single flower, its roots still firmly in the ground. He had smiled at Erika and put his index finger to a petal, saying, "She loves me." He touched every petal without plucking one blade.

Today, I parked at the first grassy mound with daisies, scaled the pasture fence, and walked up the rise. At the top, I sat quietly on the ground and listened. The sounds of mooing and tinkling cowbells drifted at me as a slight breeze bent the flowers toward the Alps. Stretched out on the cushion of green, I closed my eyes. Life-affirming spirit filled me.

A bug tickled my arm in the warming sun, and I looked at my watch. It read an hour later. I sat up and waited more minutes to feel Brian's presence or maybe even see him. Only the serenity my son loved came to me.

I sat outside the fence, pressed my folded hands to my face, and looked upward for direction. The idea that Brian might emerge among the daisies apparently came from my intense desire to find him rather than from the energy between us. I was disappointed but willing to explore any type of rendezvous. *Keep looking*, I told myself.

Down the hill at the car repair shop, I parked in front of the stall where our station wagon had been serviced forty years before and walked to the front door. Pressing my hand hard against the knob, I turned it, the memory of my long-ago hesitancy still fresh. I stepped inside the cool air and could almost see Erika and me standing beside the fan. Today, the large room displayed new cars for sale.

Behind the familiar counter stood a slightly stooped, graying man signing an invoice. Alois. I smiled in anticipation, and when he looked up, he blinked for moments before his sky-blue eyes shone. He rushed to embrace me, saying, "You look just the same."

I folded my arms around him and said, "I would recognize you anywhere." The hugs turned to furrowed brows, and the tears flowed.

After sitting down for coffee and giving each other highlights of the past forty years, Alois peered at me. "You must have come back for something important."

"I did. To meet Brian," I said.

The mechanic rubbed his eyes and studied me. I told him the mirror ball story, and he affirmed that anything is possible and offered to go with me to the river.

"Thank you," I said, "but I'm looking in other places."

His face became impassive, and he asked if I would like to drive through Fliess and see the updated guesthouse. I nodded; he signaled to his assistant, and we got into his car. When we reached the parking area, Alois talked about how happily his mother had lived there until she died a few years earlier at age ninety-seven. When we pulled into the swim center up the road, it looked like time had stopped in 1972. I reminisced how Erika had found the courage to finally take kicks and blow air to the side as she swam the width of the pool.

Alois and I had lunch together a few days later. His parting words were, "Life will happen like it is supposed to." To me, that meant, *be ready to seize every opportunity.*

The following morning, I went to the local music store down the street from the hotel. I had seen a display of recorders in the window and considered it possible that Brian might choose to come here. Standing among the wooden and plastic instruments, I picked up a Dolmetsch model that was almost like my son's. I played "You Are My Sunshine" several times. Then I fingered "Stand by Me." I showed two children who had watched and listened how to finger the recorder. While they practiced, I waited, took one more look around, and left.

I went to an elementary school playground that afternoon and sat under a tree to watch children play baseball. A game was in progress, and I tried to catch a glimpse of a blond boy who swung a bat like Brian, but no child had my son's confident swing. Back in my room, I prayed: *Dear God, what next?*

That night, I stood with people who crowded the town square

and listened to Austrian folk music. When locals danced a waltz or polka, I stepped along. A rock band came afterward, and I swung and swayed to the middle of the circle. Eventually, kids of all ages joined me. We line danced the Hokey Pokey and the twist. Regularly, I glanced about, searching for my son. I couldn't see him, but rocking and twisting brought back memories of us moving together.

After dark, I climbed to the residential streets and found Sunny waiting at a streetlamp. He curled against my chest while we visited the nooks and crannies where we had stowed the notes. All twelve were there. Sunny and I met three more times after more daily town searches and hill combing from Landeck to Nesselgarten, ending with the nightly music. We always checked on the notes.

The fifth night, the cat hissed at me the minute I reached for him. He padded to the side of the street and thumped his tail. I wiped my tears, blew him a kiss, and went back to my room.

I had to believe Sunny knew something I didn't.

Brian might not be looking for someone older than his thirty-year-old mother. I quickly discounted that idea, because he was always so perceptive—he would have no difficulty recognizing this senior who qualified for discounts.

It appeared I was missing the key message he was trying to send. But what was that?

In four days, I would leave Austria, and I emailed my friend Doug to update him. He was a tall, lean ballroom dancer and whitewater rafting guide from Colorado, who had negotiated the dangerous rapids of the Grand Canyon. He was now living at my house in Oregon. The next morning, I opened his reply. "Have you considered going on the Inn itself? A fifty-fifty conversation with River is an authentic way to find connection. It's like two dancers moving as one."

Did Doug mean to go into the actual river? Wade into the fast flow? I knew he wouldn't tell me to stand in water up to my waist and call to Brian. He meant I should paddle a raft.

I believed Brian would meet me someplace "safe and joyful." I had not even in my wildest dreams considered it would be on the mighty Inn River in a raft.

I had stood in the Inn and looked for my son. I had released half my fear of water when I learned to sail, but I had avoided the tiniest notion of going into the contentious flow. Now I would add zero paddling skill to that of zero swimming ability.

Time was running out on my thought-up options. After prayerful consideration, I decided to Trust with my soundest resolve.

Brian's message had said, *I'll be waiting.* And Doug keenly understood water's revelations and healing powers, along with what reconnecting with Brian meant to me.

TWENTY-FOUR
BRIAN

Late that morning, I drove to Sport Camp Tirol, a rafting company west of town recommended by Alois. Parking close to where the rafts and paddles were loaded, I watched elementary-school-aged children carry paddles and help adults lift rafts onto trailers. *If they take eight-year-olds, I can fit in.*

I scanned the row of buildings and found the OFFICE sign at the left end. Before I turned the knob, a tanned, muscular man in his late thirties opened the door and, with an enormous smile, grasped my hand. "Welcome. I'm Andy, the owner." Wall posters showed fit-looking young men and women paddling white water and others plunging down falls. He sensed my reluctance and understood I was not ready to hand him my credit card for a Class V rapids trip.

Andy motioned me to a chair inside the sparsely furnished room, pulled another in front, and sat down. He asked how he could help. I wiped my damp forehead, sat straight up, and took a breath. Should I start with the drowning story? Or my seven-day search following Brian's voice that called me back to Austria? He picked up on my long pause and offered his own background, telling me he had come from Great Britain twenty years before, had worked at Sport Camp Tirol for fifteen years, and had owned the company for five.

I summarized the drowning and mirror ball events, and how I had tried since childhood to learn to swim but found it beyond the ability of my non-buoyant body. "My great fear is that I will drown trying to find Brian," I said.

The sun passed over the mountains from the northeast and spread into the room. When I gave more detail about the accident, Andy brushed his hand through his hair and spoke. "You know, Janice, there's no way you could have saved Brian." He told me that when water is released from the dams upriver, the flow on the stretch of the Inn by Nesselgarten is so fast and strong that a champion swimmer could not have saved him, even considering the lower rise and slower speed in 1972. I took several deep breaths while tears soaked me.

I finally felt relief in believing I had made the tough choice that day on the river and took the last step to grace. If I had tried to reach my son, there would have been another tragedy for Erika and Oskar to bear.

Knowing my son would never jeopardize my safety, I inquired about less dangerous stretches near Nesselgarten. Andy said, "Yes, we have runs with Class II rapids for families with children and runs with III and IV. I can put you on a trip through a stretch near Imster that is Class III and IV. With a wetsuit, life vest, and helmet, you'll be perfectly safe."

Why did Andy choose this particular stretch? My trust in him had grown, and I felt he believed I could navigate this group of rapids. His experience with rafters of different motivations and skills had given him keen insight, and he seemed to understand on a deep level that my yearning was far from typical. Knowing my only swimming skill was dog-paddling, he planned to put me with Matt, his most experienced guide. He also reassured me that Austria and Sport

Camp Tirol have the highest safety standards for river rafting, and that the government continues to make them even tougher.

I stood up and shook my legs away from the clinging capris, hugged Andy, and told him I would think over what he'd said and come back tomorrow. Aware that I knew nothing about rafting, I wanted to gather basic information about expectations of me and the boat.

That evening, I looked up the criteria for Class III and IV rapids. Class III has waves to four feet and narrow passages that cause a boat to shimmy. Class IV has long, difficult rapids, narrow passages, and turbulent water. I also read information about obstacles such as rocks and what might cause a boat to flip. None of the details reassured me, but I understood the practical reality of each class. The river wasn't going to do me any favors, but something told me I could meet those requirements.

I drove back to Sport Camp Tirol the following morning and asked Andy if he had time for three more questions before I booked for the following day. He nodded.

"How long could I survive if I fell into the water?"

Andy pointed to a wetsuit hanging on a wall. "Wetsuits, life vests, helmets, and flippers keep you warm, protected, and afloat. We've never had a person drown."

I continued. "What if there is a long drop, and Matt can't see all the obstacles from above, and we plunge into one of them?"

Andy looked straight at me. "My guides have run all the stretches of this river many times. Plus, we get hourly updates to assess last-minute changes in the river."

I clasped my hands. "Good! But what if a wave at the bottom of a drop is so large it flips the boat?"

The guide's eyes narrowed, and he took my arm. "Before you leave on your trip, every safety precaution will be explained and practiced. In the rare case that the boat flips, you'll know exactly what to do."

I fished in my purse for a credit card, although I hadn't quite reached my comfort level. "Before I sign, can I buy one more question?"

Andy grinned as he put the card in the machine.

"What if the raft gets hung up on a rock just below the surface?"

He handed me back my card. "Remember, I told you Matt is my most experienced guide? He will be extra alert for problem rocks or debris and divert the boat around them. I'll ask that he seat you beside him."

I signed the credit slip and touched Andy's hand.

"See you at nine a.m. tomorrow," he said.

That evening, I stuffed short, medium, and long-sleeved shirts, a pair of pants, and a jacket into my pack, along with the required bathing suit and towel. I was certain that, at the take-out, I would need layers to warm up. Water, suntan lotion, and sunglasses bulged from the side pockets. An email to Doug detailed my plans. He responded, "So glad you're taking the plunge. Not literally, though." I chuckled in spite of my anxiety.

In the darkness, I snuggled under the comforter. Later, I tiptoed to the windows and opened one to listen to the river. Lapping waves were unusually light. I would leave the latch open and let the gentleness draw calm reassurance. The mirror ball voice had been clear, and I renewed my belief that the journey would unfold in a tailor-made fashion for Brian and me. And I had to trust Matt's competence.

Awake at five o'clock, I got up and showered, took small bites of breakfast, and rechecked my pack. At 7:30 a.m., I drove to Sport Camp Tirol and walked the perimeter of the huge parking lot. Near the oak and beech trees, I rubbed a stalk of purple heather—again and again. I was optimistic, but nervous beyond words.

I wasn't sure how Doug's term, *a conversation with River,* would unfold. Would my son appear as a person? Would I hear his voice and recognize it?

I would embrace whatever connected me to him.

Guides bustled near the buildings. Andy waved and then motioned me to follow him to the far end of the complex, where a blue van and trailer with the Sport Camp Tirol logo were parked. A raft had already been loaded. We hugged, and he put his hand on the shoulder of a strong and fit young man. "Janice, this is Matt. He will take good care of you." My guide extended his arm, and we shook hands. "You're going to handle this trip. I promise," he said. Then he told me to get into my wetsuit and pick up the other equipment I would need.

The wetsuit zipped, I went to my car and collected the pack, dangling the helmet and life vest from my arm. Outside the van, I strapped on the vest, then moved down the aisle to a vacant seat. None of the other nine rafters wore their vest, so I took mine off, reminding myself I was not the Greek goddess Styx going to her underworld river to be punished. I was a mother ready to reconnect with her son.

We headed to a put-in site at the edge of the village of Imst. After inching along a narrow road past farmhouses and fields, we pulled onto a grassy area. Everyone piled out. I caught a glimpse of the river between trees about fifty feet away. The Actual River. Matt came to take my hand, and we stepped outside.

He stood beside the flatbed in shorts and a baseball cap, put his palm into the air, and said, "Listen up, everyone." He paused and scanned each of our faces. "You'll hear that often today. Take it seriously. First, we'll unload the boat and extra gear. Then we'll gather here for the safety talk." *Safety talk. No escaping possible danger as part of the mix.*

Minutes later, paddles in hand, the group faced Matt and grew silent. I heard waves tumbling over rocks in the distance. Wetsuit in place, and grasping his paddle's handle, the guide gave directions for holding and driving the blade. He told us paddlers are the engine that moves the boat, but he would steer with oars to keep us on course.

We practiced gripping and stroking. "If you're thrown into the water, grab the lifeline and hang on. If you can't, float on your back with your feet downstream and toes to the surface." I had been assured that on this stretch of the Inn, boat flips and accidents were rare, and I reminded myself that, although I had taken every safety precaution, I had accepted the risks.

Matt finished his instructions. Paddle in one hand, I walked to the edge of the bank and slipped into my water shoes. Five fellow rafters carried the boat alongside me, and one of them reached out to drop my wooden stick inside it. It hit the rubber floor, and I grabbed the line to help guide the raft down somewhat level rocks to the water's edge. Sharp ones jabbed my feet. When a low, narrow wave hit a towering boulder a few yards from shore, I froze, tripped, and fell against the shoulder of the person ahead.

The yellow boat floated twenty feet away, and nine rafters waited on its side tubes. I stepped on one mossy stone at a time until the icy flow pushed at my calves, water shoes skidding and arms thrashing.

Stumbling to thigh-level water, I heard Matt say, "Dunk yourself, Janice, grab the lifeline, and climb aboard." I clutched the line and tossed splashes at my shoulders. Tightening my core, I lunged for the top of the thick rubber and slipped. Twice. The third time, trip mate Konrad held on to my life vest and pulled me in. I lay sprawled on the floor at the bow while cold drops ran down my face into the wetsuit. I shivered from forehead to toe.

From the back of the boat, Matt called, "Everybody, get ready to practice stroking before we enter the current. Grip the T-bar, lean forward, and dip the blade down." I scrambled upright, sat on the left front, and thrust the shaft into the water, drawing back like I had been taught. No resistance. The raft went forward without my help. I pulled back until I knew I was contributing nothing.

We approached the channel, and small waves bounced the boat. Matt said, "Paddle forward!" I reached the paddle ahead, plunged it deep, and stroked back with all my strength. Yes! The draw to midchannel was smooth, and I stroked as a team member while we skirted smaller rocks.

The boat pointed between medium-sized boulders on the left and right while I shifted to glance at Matt. "Paddle hard," he said. We turned right. "Left side, stop."

I tried to relax while five German college students shouted, "Bring on the big ones." We cut through frothy waves that spilled over the bow, hitting our legs. Thick sheets of water splashed my face, and earthy smells filled my nose. Matt said, "Hard forward," and I blew out constricted breaths. My lifelong fear of drowning filled me for a long moment.

Then the raft bounced, water sloshed over both sides, and one of the guys yelled, "Here's to Class III rapids!" My arms shook from relentless stroking, but I stayed alert for breaking curls.

Matt's voice interrupted. "Listen up. The first big rapid is ahead beyond the bridge. There's a boulder on the left, then a steep drop, and rolling waves at the bottom."

I watched murky spring melt run past the rock toward the falls.

A large rapid. If the boat flipped, and I fell in and drowned, I would have to wait to tell Brian that my love reached beyond his brief life. I couldn't let that happen.

We moved parallel to the boulder, and my paddle lay frozen

across my lap. I peered at it without recognition. The raft headed for the edge of the waterfall.

The fearful me said, *Take me to shore.*

Weren't all of my attempts to meet Brian meant to lead to this moment? The success of meeting my son rested with the courage I had built up. That confident me said, *Stay.*

I stayed.

⟿

Time and raftmates went away.

Inhaling and exhaling, I wiggled my toes. My body steadied, and I tilted my head upward.

A four-foot-tall figure wearing the familiar blue shirt and tan pants balanced against the raft's bow.

Brian.

Light beamed from eyes that danced and lips that reached toward pink cheeks. While his left arm came toward my shoulder, his right cradled the beloved Sunny cat.

I covered my mouth.

"I'm here, Mom, to say that I will love you forever, no matter what."

I leaned to within inches of him and said, "I wanted more than life itself to save you. Please forgive me that I couldn't."

Brian told me I could raft this river and do everything heartfelt.

I said, "My love for you is endless. And fathomless."

Energy surged between us, and I basked in the bliss of an eternal relationship.

I folded my hands in gratitude as his likeness faded.

⟿

"Paddle hard forward!"

Matt's voice broke through the invisible world and jolted me back to the river's rapids.

I grabbed the shaft, plunged it over the side, and stroked fast. The raft lifted and came down while wide waves scrolled across the front and sides. My mouth flooded, and I coughed and choked until I could finally breathe normally.

The guide said, "Everyone, stop."

Triumphant shouts came from the other rafters and echoed through the canyon. I rubbed my arms and felt warmth inside the wetsuit. Konrad, who had first pulled me into the boat, gave me a thumbs-up.

We floated beyond the white water, the trailing waves filling me with satisfaction and love I now could absorb. More big rapids awaited, but I savored the moment.

Matt's voice broke in to say that we would float beside the eddy for ten minutes. I dropped my paddle across my knees, shifted to the outside of the tube, and scanned the surrounding landscape. The trills of an orange-breasted chaffinch made me smile. Then my eyes caught bunches of single-winged seeds hanging from European ash trees. Brian's beloved "helicopters." I blinked a prayer to them.

The swimmers boarded the boat for the second group of rapids, Class IIIs and IVs with a narrow channel and large boulders under the surface. I thrust the blade with force and plunged and pulled, water blasts hitting my face and stopping my breath. Inhaling and letting air out as often as I could, I ignored my stinging eyes.

Matt's voice sounded above the excitement, "Listen up. You'll need your best skills for the last set of rapids. They are Class IV with rocky, constricted channels, large waves, and long drops."

Andy had promised I could sit in the back beside Matt, and I had kept that option open. When I landed on the boat floor earlier, I was too frozen in fear to move. Yet besides learning to trust myself and God in small steps, Brian had assured me I could raft this river. I wanted the full sense of accomplishment with the Class IV challenge, a portion of my energy coming from the thrill of the unknown.

"Both sides paddle hard forward. And don't let go. *Now!*"

The first big rapid churned close to the front of the raft. I crammed my toes into the toe pocket and drove my paddle through the racing water. We skidded over the first hole. When the boat hit the vertical chain of standing waves, it pointed upward, then fell.

"Harder, faster."

I plunged the blade until I leaned dangerously over the edge.

"Stronger. Dig!"

At full power, my body stayed locked in concentration while we slid past holes and punched through others. The raft bounced forward and sideways with stretches of recirculating water and froth slapping back upstream. Chest flaming, I stroked as if my life depended on this skill set. In one sense, it did.

Waves struck and covered the raft as it tumbled downward, almost knocking me to the floor. Only my foot, pushed against the toe pocket, kept me stable.

It felt like a split-second and forever before the boat leveled over the tail waves and coasted. Water washed down my face, and I cheered the confidence to navigate a river. And life.

I jumped up and touched my paddle blade with the other rafters. Laughter came from the take-out site ahead, and I slid over the center tubes to sit beside Matt. I hugged him and said, "Thank you."

An ash seed landed near my foot. I picked up the little helicopter, kissed it, and sent it into the wind.

TWENTY-FIVE
RETURNING FEELINGS

The raft had been pulled onto the grassy area, and I sat on its edge in T-shirt and shorts. Afternoon sun invited me to stroke my paddle backward several times—easy when there's no water to push. The river's moderate and steady downstream flow felt reassuring, with plants and animals in its wetness continuing to restore themselves and their environment.

I have profound gratitude for the moments I spent meditating in the hillsides and field of daisies where I felt Brian's love for his sister. The opportunity to play the recorder for smiling children was a reminder of the instrument's connection to my son's world. A boy swinging his bat and watching the ball fly skyward took me to the memory of my son's home-run hits. And my Sunny friend validated the animal world's soulful knowing once more.

Following the tragedy, my goal was to help my family recover, keep my own body and soul afloat, and honor Brian's memory. I saw my son as God's intermediary with strength to uplift us all.

I have no reason to float the Inn River again. Whether I am traveling the planet alone or with others, hiking through a forest in Oregon, or dancing tango in Argentina, I will know my son is beside me.

Although our meeting on the river could not have been further from my original goal, the Higher Power knew that Brian could help me address the deepest issues related to the drowning. My long restorative process awarded me a firm belief in myself, keener trust in God, and the anticipation of further mysteries waiting to unfurl.

It was time to put my new energy to practical use. I never expected to work out every detail of every issue regarding Brian or other family members, but I was determined to be more introspective concerning others' personal struggles. Knowing that people face difficulties they can't even describe gives me the patience to honor their attempts. Immense joy can be had by trying. And the more someone tries, the greater the chance of a successful outcome.

My friend Doug will continue to have an important place in my life. Why wouldn't he—the man who offered that partner dancing could connect me with Brian? I had met him on a dance floor, and our friendship grew. We had taken Class II Willamette River trips together in his raft, but he was clear that those rapids were no match for the Inn's. I hold dear his confidence that I could handle the trip.

I had become a person who engaged with both the potentials and hazards of water, transforming from a non-swimming child who feared drowning to a mother who talked with her son on a river in white water.

I will never completely let go of memories of the drowning, but I can now view the Inn River with confidence and skill as a transforming force. My spirit has been renewed.

The day before I left Austria, I had lunch with a lovely couple who live in the general area of the accident. Ulli's husband had taken me to visit two dams along the Inn to add details of the river's flow. Over plates of *spargel*—white asparagus topped with butter, sprinkled with lemon, and served with boiled potatoes—Ulli expressed how, as a mother, she understood my reunion with Brian as one of *filling up my heart once again.*

I returned to the US and the home I had lived in since 2002. Dropping my luggage, I hurried to my office desk to view the photo of the four of us and confirm the hope I was feeling. Instead, the photo felt cold and foreign. Turning on the light near a living room bookshelf that contained titles my children and I had read together, I stared at the spines. I saw words without meaning. Catching the shine of Brian's recorder, my mind portrayed him playing a fading melody instead of the usual relevant tune.

My son seemed to have left my presence, and I missed him just as much as in 1972 when I had faced life without him. I walked a path in my backwoods and sobbed, trying to sense Brian again. Finally, I went back inside without a hint of guidance.

By chance, I opened an email from Ulli. She wrote about a doctor friend who, during hospice children's care, found that when kids know they will die, they develop deep wisdom, even if time is short. Their eyes show they desire to free their families to live life abundantly. The doctor said, "A child relaxes and comes to peace when he knows his family understands his message."

These words were both jolting and comforting. I thought back to my son's last moments clinging to the boulder. Although I was a distance away, I had caught Brian's expressions. When he first looked straight at Oskar and me, his cheeks were taut, his mouth was wide, and his eyes appeared wild. Then, the second before he left the rock, his whole being relaxed and his face said, "I will be fine."

I looked again at the photo. The faces were all reflective, reassuring me one more time that Brian is at peace forever.

We grieve because we seek to give and receive love, with the hope that sad memories find their rightful place among the happy ones. I will never be privy to even half of Oskar's thoughts or questions along his life journey. Fortunately, Brian and I talked a lot during his short life, and Erika and I continue to share opinions and feelings today.

The four of us have eternal love in common.

A few weeks ago, I received this message and a photo from Ulli:

". . . remembering Brian . . . we cycled along the Inn River, and I threw some elderflowers into the water for him from that wooden bridge located about eighty meters downstream from the Mayr auto repair shop. We are fortunate to be alive."

One day, Ulli and I will take a bike ride along the Inn River. If it is in the spring, the refreshing air, the water's root system nourishment, and the sun will combine to form leaves that fill branches. We will welcome their beauty.

If in the fall, the crisp air, green water, and breezes will flutter the orange and yellow shapes toward the stream. We will welcome their color and journey to decompose and enrich.

TWENTY-SIX
FORGIVENESS

After I returned from Austria, I visited the retired Oskar at the townhouse where Erika had moved him to make alcohol access difficult and to allow home care for his developing dementia. With his life and memory difficulties, we weren't comfortable with telling him I had met Brian in Austria. As a traveler himself in times past who was interested in others' experiences, I would ordinarily have given a brief travelogue of my time in Jordan and Israel.

But today, when I told him I had been away awhile, his eyes quickly went from blinking at me to picking up the TV remote and clicking it on. Possibly, talk of a trip brought unwanted memories of the accident. Years after the divorce, when Oskar traveled solo to Russia and Norway, Erika and I prayed that he would find some resolution and peace. We never saw that happen.

I offered to augment the hired assistance and bring a meal twice a week. The first Tuesday, recalling his lifetime delight for an open-faced sandwich with carrot and pea salad, I served him a plate with three sandwiches, a banana, and sparkling water. He gobbled the food, asked for more, and again riveted his eyes on the TV.

The next time I visited, he was surprisingly lucid, and I ventured to say once more, "You are not responsible for Brian's drowning. Your whole being wanted to save him. Life happens, and God knows that."

He seemed to understand, rubbed a bit of moisture from his eyes, and turned back to the TV. I was happy Oskar could take a small momentary step away from his grief, guilt, and pain. One day, two years later, I found him unusually alert despite his accelerating cognitive decline. I sat close, took his hand, and asked forgiveness for any hurt I had caused him. His eyes softened, and his hand pressed against mine. Eyes wide now, I asked him to squeeze my palm if he understood. His fingers closed over mine, and he kept them there. I felt energy flow through every muscle. We had reached the summit of our journey along paths with both joyful family adventures and rocky cliffs. I believe God knew Oskar needed this closure and granted him these moments of clarity.

Erika and I had lunch after visiting Oskar one day and asked for in-depth forgiveness of problems we had needed more perspective to address. I told her I had quit counting my mistakes as her mother, and she reassured me she had "forgotten them." She said she honored me for the love and dedication I gave her, her brother, and her dad. I hugged her tightly and said, "Sweetie, I never dreamed I would have a daughter as wonderful as you."

In August 2018, as I approached Oskar's hospice bed, his head was turned to the wall. Rubbing his arm, I said, "It's Jan." When he looked at me without expression, I asked him how old he was. No response.

I ran my hand through his hair. It had gone from blond to chestnut brown, and his skin had become a darker shade to match. I bent nearer, took his hand, and one last time said, "You did your best for Brian, for Erika, and for me. For that, I will always love you."

I smiled and asked again, "When is your birthday?"

His eyes blinked with the exact day, month, and year.

Erika walked slowly to her father's bedside and straightened his pillow. She leaned close and kissed his cheek while her tears fell. She said, "You saved my life that day at the river. I love you, Dad." I stood at the foot of the bed and watched the years of tension between them dissolve. Oskar's half-lidded eyes met hers, and although no further words were spoken, he seemed to embrace the principled and competent woman she was. Erika told me later, "It's been a long goodbye, but I was able to say all that was loving and good within my heart."

Oskar passed away the next morning. The verse, 1 John 4:18, came to mind: "Perfect love drives out fear."

In the afternoon, Erika, Tim, our longtime friend Dan, and I sat at an outdoor restaurant along the Willamette River. The alder and maple trees shaded our table, and the birches bent toward the water, creating a soothing backdrop for our celebration of life.

We ordered an appetizer called honey-lemon whipped goat cheese on toast. At his seventy-fifth catered birthday celebration for family and friends, Oskar had chosen goat cheese for open-faced sandwiches, goat cheese on crostini with greens, and goat cheese molded into cheese balls.

The four of us chewed slowly and thoughtfully as we reflected on treasured times with the man who believed this cheese to be the ideal gift of affection.

TWENTY-SEVEN
JOY

The rivers flow not past, but through us, thrilling, tingling, vibrating every fiber and cell of the substance of our bodies, making them glide and sing.

—John Muir

River's tingling spirit courses through me every day.

At tranquil times, when the tiniest ripple tickles my toes with pleasure, I watch my son play among the agates and trout. I scoop water, splash it over myself, and reach my arms outward. His zest for life enfolds me.

When routine whitecaps send moderate obstacles my way, I remember how Brian took the surges of life in stride. If an alternate paddle or different stroke is called for, I embrace the rises and falls of a new rhythm. My son fills me with enthusiasm for the challenge.

When the waves turn too wild to navigate, I hang out in an eddy and point my hands upward.

The water calms and rolls downstream. Mist rises to send energy through me, allowing my inner light to sing.

I move forward with heartfelt boldness.

ACKNOWLEDGMENTS

After I returned from my second trip to the Inn River in 2012—forty years after the first—my friend Opal Powell urged me to set down the incredible rendezvous with my son. Teacher Linda Clare's encouragement led to my submission of "A Voice from the River" and its acceptance for the 2013 book, *Chicken Soup for the Soul: Miraculous Messages from Heaven.*

Three years later, motivated by the desire to help others find a healing path, colleague Mary Bauer and I wrote journals, made notes, and finally, each shared a first version of a full memoir. I am indebted to Mary for her candid and introspective input through several iterations, and for her unwavering dedication to the long process.

Writing instructor and author Debra Gwartney taught us both how to organize topics, structure chapters, and bring emotion to the page.

I offer my sincere thank-you to writer-teachers Jay Ponterri, Pam Houston, Fenton Johnson, Laura McCaffrey, and Sandra Scofield, who gave prized editing suggestions.

Beta Readers Karen Antikajian, Ruthy Kanagy, Marisela Rizik, Karen Mack, Kadri Jacobsen, and Jillian Smith, read the manuscript for overall content and, without exception, offered encouraging input. Jason Maurer provided valuable and specific critiques of each chapter.

Rebecca Ivanoff and Dr. Barbara Mossberg read the final draft, their energy taking me to the last word change.

Alice Cura's final proofreading was exceptionally detailed and thorough. Thank you.

In 2023, I was directed to Brooke Warner at She Writes Press, a wellspring for women writers. Brooke believed in my story and guided it to publication.

I honor and cherish each family member and friend who stood with us through the small and large challenges. Your patience and enduring care speak to me today.

I also have enormous praise for my personal friends around the world—every one of you stayed close both during the years of recovery and my movement forward. This list includes the teachers and members of local and international dance communities.

A huge debt of gratitude to Doug Lee, who believed I could navigate the Class IV rapids of the Inn River. Let's have a dance in celebration!

Lovely Austrian friend, Ulli—you traveled with me through every bend and kind of water detailed in this book, and through all that's happened in real time since we met in 2012. I can't wait for your next email with another recounting of peaceful moments on the Inn. I am honored to consider you a soul sister.

There will never be another foursome or threesome like my family. The nucleus of my heart includes the four of us and always will. I am in awe of the many sunny experiences we had together, but also the gloomy ones when we could hold hands and ford the ripples.

Steering through ripples one by one led me to celebrate the joy I cherish today.

ABOUT THE AUTHOR

photo credit:
Heather Mills Photography

While working as an educator and author in Syria, Colombia, Saudi Arabia, Oregon, and Washington, **Janice Jensen** embarked on a decades-long journey to glean insights from parents who had lost children. While traveling solo to seventy countries, she examined the grief experiences of several cultures and identities, leading her to embrace a vast range of strategies for overcoming tragedy. *One Ripple at a Time* incorporates the best of her brain and heart wisdom, and today, she lives in Oregon and volunteers with groups to give informal grief recovery support and pass on strength for a thriving life.

Janice loves to hear from her readers. Visit her website at janicejensenauthor.com.

Looking for your next great read?

We can help!

Visit www.shewritespress.com/next-read
or scan the QR code below for a list
of our recommended titles.

She Writes Press is an award-winning
independent publishing company founded to
serve women writers everywhere.